MznLnx

Missing Links Exam Preps

Exam Prep for

Introduction To Operations And Supply Chain Management

Bozarth, Handfield, 1st Edition

The MznLnx Exam Prep is your link from the texbook and lecture to your exams.
The MznLnx Exam Preps are unauthorized and comprehensive reviews of your textbooks.

All material provided by MznLnx and Rico Publications (c) 2010
Textbook publishers and textbook authors do not particpate in or contribute to these reviews.

MznLnx

Rico
Publications

Exam Prep for Introduction To Operations And Supply Chain Management
1st Edition
Bozarth, Handfield

Publisher: Raymond Houge
Assistant Editor: Michael Rouger
Text and Cover Designer: Lisa Buckner
Marketing Manager: Sara Swagger
Project Manager, Editorial Production: Jerry Emerson
Art Director: Vernon Lowerui

Product Manager: Dave Mason
Editorial Assitant: Rachel Guzmanji
Pedagogy: Debra Long
Cover Image: Jim Reed/Getty Images
Text and Cover Printer: City Printing, Inc.
Compositor: Media Mix, Inc.

(c) 2010 Rico Publications

ALL RIGHTS RESERVED. No part of this work covered by the copyright may be reproduced or used in any form or by an means--graphic, electronic, or mechanical, including photocopying, recording, taping, Web distribution, information storage, and retrieval systems, or in any other manner--without the written permission of the publisher.

Printed in the United States
ISBN:

For more information about our products, contact us at:
Dave.Mason@RicoPublications.com

For permission to use material from this text or product, submit a request online to:
Dave.Mason@RicoPublications.com

Contents

CHAPTER 1
Introduction to Operations and Supply Chain Management — 1

CHAPTER 2
Operations and Supply Chain Strategies — 8

CHAPTER 3
Business Processes — 14

CHAPTER 4
Managing Quality — 19

CHAPTER 5
Managing Projects — 30

CHAPTER 6
Developing Products and Services — 32

CHAPTER 7
Process Choice and Layout Decisions in Manufacturing and Services — 37

CHAPTER 8
Managing Capacity — 42

CHAPTER 9
Forecasting — 46

CHAPTER 10
Sourcing Decisions and the Purchasing Process — 52

CHAPTER 11
Logistics — 64

CHAPTER 12
Sales and Operations Planning (Aggregate Planning) — 71

CHAPTER 13
Managing Inventory throughout the Supply Chain — 78

CHAPTER 14
Managing Production across the Supply Chain — 82

CHAPTER 15
JIT/Lean Production — 86

CHAPTER 16
Managing Information Technologies across the Supply Chain — 88

ANSWER KEY — 92

TO THE STUDENT

COMPREHENSIVE

The *MznLnx* Exam Prep series is designed to help you pass your exams. Editors at MznLnx review your textbooks and then prepare these practice exams to help you master the textbook material. Unlike study guides, workbooks, and practice tests provided by the texbook publisher and textbook authors, *MznLnx* gives you **all** of the material in each chapter in exam form, not just samples, so you can be sure to nail your exam.

MECHANICAL

The MznLnx Exam Prep series creates exams that will help you learn the subject matter as well as test you on your understanding. Each question is designed to help you master the concept. Just working through the exams, you gain an understanding of the subject--its a simple mechanical process that produces success.

INTEGRATED STUDY GUIDE AND REVIEW

MznLnx is not just a set of exams designed to test you, its also a comprehensive review of the subject content. Each exam question is also a review of the concept, making sure that you will get the answer correct without having to go to other sources of material. You learn as you go! Its the easiest way to pass an exam.

HUMOR

Studying can be tedious and dry. MznLnx's instructional design includes moderate humor within the exam questions on occassion, to break the tedium and revitalize the brain

Chapter 1. Introduction to Operations and Supply Chain Management

1. _____ is a company-wide computer software system used to manage and coordinate all the resources, information, and functions of a business from shared data stores.

An _____ system has a service-oriented architecture with modular hardware and software units and 'services' that communicate on a local area network. The modular design allows a business to add or reconfigure modules (perhaps from different vendors) while preserving data integrity in one shared database that may be centralized or distributed.

   a. AAAI
   b. A4e
   c. Enterprise resource planning
   d. A Stake in the Outcome

2. A _____ is the system of organizations, people, technology, activities, information and resources involved in moving a product or service from supplier to customer. _____ activities transform natural resources, raw materials and components into a finished product that is delivered to the end customer. In sophisticated _____ systems, used products may re-enter the _____ at any point where residual value is recyclable.
   a. Drop shipping
   b. Wholesalers
   c. Supply chain
   d. Packaging

3. _____ is a term defined by the Oxford English Dictionary as an individual's 'course or progress through life '. It is usually considered to pertain to remunerative work (and sometimes also formal education.)

The etymology of the term is somewhat ironic in that it comes from the Latin word carrera, which means race .

   a. Career
   b. Spatial mismatch
   c. Career planning
   d. Nursing shortage

4. _____ is the management of a network of interconnected businesses involved in the ultimate provision of product and service packages required by end customers (Harland, 1996.) _____ spans all movement and storage of raw materials, work-in-process inventory, and finished goods from point of origin to point of consumption (supply chain.)

The definition an American professional association put forward is that _____ encompasses the planning and management of all activities involved in sourcing, procurement, conversion, and logistics management activities.

Chapter 1. Introduction to Operations and Supply Chain Management

a. Packaging
b. Supply chain management
c. Freight forwarder
d. Drop shipping

5. _____ is an area of business concerned with the production of goods and services, and involves the responsibility of ensuring that business operations are efficient in terms of using as little resource as needed, and effective in terms of meeting customer requirements. It is concerned with managing the process that converts inputs (in the forms of materials, labour and energy) into outputs (in the form of goods and services.)

Operations traditionally refers to the production of goods and services separately, although the distinction between these two main types of operations is increasingly difficult to make as manufacturers tend to merge product and service offerings.

a. A4e
b. AAAI
c. A Stake in the Outcome
d. Operations management

6. _____ in manufacturing refers to processes that occur later on in a production sequence or production line.

Viewing a company 'from order to cash' might have high-level processes such as Marketing, Sales, Order Entry, Manufacturing, Packaging, Shipping, Invoicing. Each of these could be deconstructed into many sub-processes and supporting processes.

a. Science Learning Centre
b. Probability-generating function
c. Genbutsu
d. Downstream

7. A _____ is a commercial building for storage of goods. _____s are used by manufacturers, importers, exporters, wholesalers, transport businesses, customs, etc. They are usually large plain buildings in industrial areas of cities and towns.
a. 1990 Clean Air Act
b. 28-hour day
c. Warehouse
d. 33 Strategies of War

Chapter 1. Introduction to Operations and Supply Chain Management 3

8. _____, commonly known as e-commerce, consists of the buying and selling of products or services over electronic systems such as the Internet and other computer networks. The amount of trade conducted electronically has grown extraordinarily with widespread Internet usage. The use of commerce is conducted in this way, spurring and drawing on innovations in electronic funds transfer, supply chain management, Internet marketing, online transaction processing, electronic data interchange (EDI), inventory management systems, and automated data collection systems.

   a. A Stake in the Outcome
   b. Electronic commerce
   c. A4e
   d. Online shopping

9. _____ in its literal sense is the process of transformation of local or regional phenomena into global ones. It can be described as a process by which the people of the world are unified into a single society and function together.

This process is a combination of economic, technological, sociocultural and political forces.

   a. Histogram
   b. Cost Management
   c. Globalization
   d. Collaborative Planning, Forecasting and Replenishment

10. _____ is a Fortune 500, American multinational corporation headquartered in Cincinnati, Ohio, that manufactures a wide range of consumer goods. As of 2008, P'G is the 8th largest corporation in the world by market capitalization and 14th largest US company by profit.

   a. Maturity of Organizations and Business Excellence - The Four-Phase Model
   b. Turnover
   c. Procter ' Gamble Co.
   d. STAR

11. A _____ is something for which there is demand, but which is supplied without qualitative differentiation across a market. It is a product that is the same no matter who produces it, such as petroleum, notebook paper, or milk. In other words, copper is copper.

   a. 28-hour day
   b. 1990 Clean Air Act
   c. 33 Strategies of War
   d. Commodity

12. _____ is the provision of service to customers before, during and after a purchase.

Chapter 1. Introduction to Operations and Supply Chain Management

According to Turban et al. (2002), '_____ is a series of activities designed to enhance the level of customer satisfaction - that is, the feeling that a product or service has met the customer expectation.'

Its importance varies by product, industry and customer; defective or broken merchandise can be exchanged, often only with a receipt and within a specified time frame.

a. 28-hour day
b. 1990 Clean Air Act
c. Customer service
d. Service rate

13. The _____ is a not-for-profit United States association for the benefit of the purchasing and supply management profession, particularly in the areas of education and research.

It was founded in 1913 as the New York Association of Purchasing Management after a purchasing meeting organized by the Thomas Register. It was established in 1915 as the National Association of Purchasing Management.

a. Institute for Supply Management
b. A Stake in the Outcome
c. AAAI
d. A4e

14. _____ is the management of the flow of goods, information and other resources, including energy and people, between the point of origin and the point of consumption in order to meet the requirements of consumers (frequently, and originally, military organizations.) _____ involves the integration of information, transportation, inventory, warehousing, material-handling, and packaging, and occasionally security. _____ is a channel of the supply chain which adds the value of time and place utility.

a. Third-party logistics
b. 28-hour day
c. 1990 Clean Air Act
d. Logistics

15. A _____ is an employee within a company, business or other organization who is responsible at some level for buying or approving the acquisition of goods and services needed by the company. The position responsibilities may be the same as that of a buyer or purchasing agent, or may include wider supervisory or managerial responsibilities. A _____ may oversee the acquisition of materials needed for production, general supplies for offices and facilities, equipment, or construction contracts.

a. Financial analyst
b. Director of communications
c. CEO
d. Purchasing manager

16. _____ is an advertisement in which a particular product specifically mentions a competitor by name for the express purpose of showing why the competitor is inferior to the product naming it.

This should not be confused with parody advertisements, where a fictional product is being advertised for the purpose of poking fun at the particular advertisement, nor should it be confused with the use of a coined brand name for the purpose of comparing the product without actually naming an actual competitor. ('Wikipedia tastes better and is less filling than the Encyclopedia Galactica.')

In the 1980s, during what has been referred to as the cola wars, soft-drink manufacturer Pepsi ran a series of advertisements where people, caught on hidden camera, in a blind taste test, chose Pepsi over rival Coca-Cola.

a. Comparative advertising
b. 1990 Clean Air Act
c. 33 Strategies of War
d. 28-hour day

17. _____ is the process of determining the production capacity needed by an organization to meet changing demands for its products. In the context of _____, 'capacity' is the maximum amount of work that an organization is capable of completing in a given period of time.

A discrepancy between the capacity of an organization and the demands of its customers results in inefficiency, either in under-utilized resources or unfulfilled customers.

a. Scientific management
b. Productivity
c. Remanufacturing
d. Capacity planning

18. _____ is the process of estimation in unknown situations. Prediction is a similar, but more general term. Both can refer to estimation of time series, cross-sectional or longitudinal data.

a. 28-hour day
b. 33 Strategies of War
c. Forecasting
d. 1990 Clean Air Act

19. The term _____ is that part of Supply Chain Management that plans, implements, and controls the efficient, effective, forward, and reverse flow and storage of goods, services, and related information between the point of origin and the point of consumption in order to meet customers' requirements.

Software is used for logistics automation which helps the supply chain industry in automating the work flow as well as management of the system. There are very few generalized software available in the new market in the said topology.

a. Dynamic Enterprise Modeling
b. Micromanagement
c. Logistics Management
d. Contingency theory

20. _____ is one of the managerial functions like planning, organizing, staffing and directing. It is an important function because it helps to check the errors and to take the corrective action so that deviation from standards are minimized and stated goals of the organization are achieved in desired manner. According to modern concepts, _____ is a foreseeing action whereas earlier concept of _____ was used only when errors were detected. _____ in management means setting standards, measuring actual performance and taking corrective action.

a. Decision tree pruning
b. Turnover
c. Schedule of reinforcement
d. Control

21. _____ is a term used to describe practice of sourcing from the global market for goods and services across geopolitical boundaries. _____ often aims to exploit global efficiencies in the delivery of a product or service. These efficiencies include low cost skilled labor, low cost raw material and other economic factors like tax breaks and low trade tariffs.

a. Purchase requisition
b. 1990 Clean Air Act
c. Purchasing process
d. Global sourcing

Chapter 1. Introduction to Operations and Supply Chain Management

22. In business, the term word _____ refers to a number of procurement practices, aimed at finding, evaluating and engaging suppliers of goods and services:

- Global _____, a procurement strategy aimed at exploiting global efficiencies in production
- Strategic _____, a component of supply chain management, for improving and re-evaluating purchasing activities
- _____, the identification of job candidates through proactive recruiting technique
- Co-_____, a type of auditing service
- Low-cost country _____, a procurement strategy for acquiring materials from countries with lower labour and production costs in order to cut operating expenses
- Corporate _____, a supply chain, purchasing/procurement, and inventory function
- Second-tier _____, a practice of rewarding suppliers for attempting to achieve minority-owned business spending goals of their customer
- Netsourcing, a practice of utilizing an established group of businesses, individuals, or hardware ' software applications to streamline or initiate procurement practices by tapping in to and working through a third party provider
- Inverted _____, a price volatility reduction strategy usually conducted by procurement or supply-chain person by which the value of an organization's waste-stream is maximized by actively seeking out the highest price possible from a range of potential buyers exploiting price trends and other market factors
- Multisourcing, a strategy that treats a given function, such as IT, as a portfolio of activities, some of which should be outsourced and others of which should be performed by internal staff.
- Crowdsourcing, using an undefined, generally large group of people or community in the form of an open call to perform a task

In journalism, it can also refer to:

- Journalism _____, the practice of identifying a person or publication that gives information
- Single _____, the reuse of content in publishing

In computing, it can refer to:

- Open-_____, the act of releasing previously proprietary software under an open source/free software license
- Power _____ equipment, network devices that will provide power in a Power over Ethernet (PoE) setup

a. Continuous
b. Reinforcement
c. Cost Management
d. Sourcing

Chapter 2. Operations and Supply Chain Strategies

1. _____ is subcontracting a process, such as product design or manufacturing, to a third-party company. The decision to outsource is often made in the interest of lowering cost or making better use of time and energy costs, redirecting or conserving energy directed at the competencies of a particular business, or to make more efficient use of land, labor, capital, (information) technology and resources. _____ became part of the business lexicon during the 1980s.
    a. Operant conditioning
    b. Unemployment insurance
    c. Opinion leadership
    d. Outsourcing

2. A _____ is a computer program typically used to provide some form of artificial intelligence, which consists primarily of a set of rules about behavior. These rules, termed productions, are a basic representation found useful in AI planning, expert systems and action selection. A _____ provides the mechanism necessary to execute productions in order to achieve some goal for the system.
    a. 28-hour day
    b. 33 Strategies of War
    c. 1990 Clean Air Act
    d. Production system

3. _____ is an advertisement in which a particular product specifically mentions a competitor by name for the express purpose of showing why the competitor is inferior to the product naming it.

This should not be confused with parody advertisements, where a fictional product is being advertised for the purpose of poking fun at the particular advertisement, nor should it be confused with the use of a coined brand name for the purpose of comparing the product without actually naming an actual competitor. ('Wikipedia tastes better and is less filling than the Encyclopedia Galactica.')

In the 1980s, during what has been referred to as the cola wars, soft-drink manufacturer Pepsi ran a series of advertisements where people, caught on hidden camera, in a blind taste test, chose Pepsi over rival Coca-Cola.

    a. 33 Strategies of War
    b. Comparative advertising
    c. 1990 Clean Air Act
    d. 28-hour day

4. _____ is a business management strategy aimed at embedding awareness of quality in all organizational processes. _____ has been widely used in manufacturing, education, hospitals, call centers, government, and service industries, as well as NASA space and science programs.

Chapter 2. Operations and Supply Chain Strategies

As defined by the International Organization for Standardization (ISO):

'_____ is a management approach for an organization, centered on quality, based on the participation of all its members and aiming at long-term success through customer satisfaction, and benefits to all members of the organization and to society.' ISO 8402:1994

One major aim is to reduce variation from every process so that greater consistency of effort is obtained. (Royse, D., Thyer, B., Padgett D., ' Logan T., 2006)

a. 28-hour day
b. 1990 Clean Air Act
c. Quality management
d. Total quality management

5. _____ can be considered to have three main components: quality control, quality assurance and quality improvement. _____ is focused not only on product quality, but also the means to achieve it. _____ therefore uses quality assurance and control of processes as well as products to achieve more consistent quality.
   a. Quality management
   b. 1990 Clean Air Act
   c. 28-hour day
   d. Total quality management

6. _____ refers to the aggregated strategies of single business firm or a strategic business unit (SBU) in a diversified corporation. According to Michael Porter, a firm must formulate a _____ that incorporates either cost leadership, differentiation or focus in order to achieve a sustainable competitive advantage and long-term success in its chosen arenas or industries.

Functional strategies include marketing strategies, new product development strategies, human resource strategies, financial strategies, legal strategies, supply-chain strategies, and information technology management strategies.

   a. Switching cost
   b. Competitive heterogeneity
   c. Business strategy
   d. Strategic thinking

7. _____ is something that a firm can do well and that meets the following three conditions:

Chapter 2. Operations and Supply Chain Strategies

Competencies are things that companys execute well across several business units or product sectors.

Firms usually have few competencies, but these are usually less liable to change rapidly.

1. It provides consumer benefits
2. It is not easy for competitors to imitate
3. It can be leveraged widely to many products and markets.

A _____ can take various forms, including technical/subject matter know-how, a reliable process and/or close relationships with customers and suppliers (Mascarenhas et al. 1998.)

   a. NAIRU
   b. Dominant Design
   c. Learning-by-doing
   d. Core competency

8. _____ refers to the overarching strategy of the diversified firm. Such a _____ answers the questions of 'in which businesses should we be in?' and 'how does being in these business create synergy and/or add to the competitive advantage of the corporation as a whole?'

Business strategy refers to the aggregated strategies of single business firm or a strategic business unit (SBU) in a diversified corporation. According to Michael Porter, a firm must formulate a business strategy that incorporates either cost leadership, differentiation or focus in order to achieve a sustainable competitive advantage and long-term success in its chosen arenas or industries.

   a. Strategic group
   b. Competitive heterogeneity
   c. Corporate strategy
   d. Strategic drift

9. A _____ is a brief written statement of the purpose of a company or organization. Ideally, a _____ guides the actions of the organization, spells out its overall goal, provides a sense of direction, and guides decision making for all levels of management.

_____s often contain the following:

- Purpose and aim of the organization
- The organization's primary stakeholders: clients, stockholders, etc.
- Responsibilities of the organization toward these stakeholders
- Products and services offered

In developing a _____:

- Encourage as much input as feasible from employees, volunteers, and other stakeholders
- Publicize it broadly

The _____ can be used to resolve differences between business stakeholders. Stakeholders include: employees including managers and executives, stockholders, board of directors, customers, suppliers, distributors, creditors, governments (local, state, federal, etc.), unions, competitors, NGO's, and the general public.

a. 33 Strategies of War
b. 1990 Clean Air Act
c. Mission statement
d. 28-hour day

10. A _____ is the system of organizations, people, technology, activities, information and resources involved in moving a product or service from supplier to customer. _____ activities transform natural resources, raw materials and components into a finished product that is delivered to the end customer. In sophisticated _____ systems, used products may re-enter the _____ at any point where residual value is recyclable.
   a. Packaging
   b. Drop shipping
   c. Supply chain
   d. Wholesalers

11. In economics, business, retail, and accounting, a _____ is the value of money that has been used up to produce something, and hence is not available for use anymore. In economics, a _____ is an alternative that is given up as a result of a decision. In business, the _____ may be one of acquisition, in which case the amount of money expended to acquire it is counted as _____.

a. Cost allocation
b. Cost
c. Cost overrun
d. Fixed costs

12. In business and engineering, _____ is the term used to describe the complete process of bringing a new product or service to market. There are two parallel paths involved in the _____ process: one involves the idea generation, product design, and detail engineering; the other involves market research and marketing analysis. Companies typically see _____ as the first stage in generating and commercializing new products within the overall strategic process of product life cycle management used to maintain or grow their market share.

a. 28-hour day
b. 33 Strategies of War
c. New product development
d. 1990 Clean Air Act

13. In business and engineering, new _____ is the term used to describe the complete process of bringing a new product or service to market. There are two parallel paths involved in the NProduct development process: one involves the idea generation, product design, and detail engineering; the other involves market research and marketing analysis. Companies typically see new _____ as the first stage in generating and commercializing new products within the overall strategic process of product life cycle management used to maintain or grow their market share.

a. 1990 Clean Air Act
b. Product development
c. 28-hour day
d. 33 Strategies of War

14. _____ is a practice in logistics of unloading materials from an incoming semi-trailer truck or rail car and loading these materials directly into outbound trucks, trailers with little or no storage in between. This may be done to change type of conveyance, to sort material intended for different destinations or similar destination.

Cross-Dock operations were first pioneered in the US trucking industry in the 1930's, and have been in continuous use in LTL (less than truckload) operations ever since.

a. Product life cycle
b. Small business
c. Corporate recovery
d. Cross-docking

15. _____ is one of the four elements of marketing mix. An organization or set of organizations (go-betweens) involved in the process of making a product or service available for use or consumption by a consumer or business user.

The other three parts of the marketing mix are product, pricing, and promotion.

　a. Job creation programs
　b. Missing completely at random
　c. Matching theory
　d. Distribution

16. A _____ for a set of products is a warehouse or other specialized building, often with refrigeration or air conditioning, which is stocked with products (goods) to be re-distributed to retailers, wholesalers or directly to consumers. A _____ is a principle part, the 'order processing' element, of the entire 'order fulfillment' process. _____s are usually thought of as being 'demand driven'.
　a. 1990 Clean Air Act
　b. Third-party logistics
　c. 28-hour day
　d. Distribution center

Chapter 3. Business Processes

1. _____ is a Fortune 500, American multinational corporation headquartered in Cincinnati, Ohio, that manufactures a wide range of consumer goods. As of 2008, P'G is the 8th largest corporation in the world by market capitalization and 14th largest US company by profit.

    a. Maturity of Organizations and Business Excellence - The Four-Phase Model
    b. Procter ' Gamble Co.
    c. Turnover
    d. STAR

2. _____ is the management of the flow of goods, information and other resources, including energy and people, between the point of origin and the point of consumption in order to meet the requirements of consumers (frequently, and originally, military organizations.) _____ involves the integration of information, transportation, inventory, warehousing, material-handling, and packaging, and occasionally security. _____ is a channel of the supply chain which adds the value of time and place utility.

    a. 28-hour day
    b. Third-party logistics
    c. 1990 Clean Air Act
    d. Logistics

3. A _____ or business method is a collection of related, structured activities or tasks that produce a specific service or product (serve a particular goal) for a particular customer or customers. It often can be visualized with a flowchart as a sequence of activities.

    There are three types of _____es:

    1. Management processes, the processes that govern the operation of a system. Typical management processes include 'Corporate Governance' and 'Strategic Management'.
    2. Operational processes, processes that constitute the core business and create the primary value stream. Typical operational processes are Purchasing, Manufacturing, Marketing, and Sales.
    3. Supporting processes, which support the core processes. Examples include Accounting, Recruitment, Technical support.

    A _____ begins with a customer's need and ends with a customer's need fulfillment. Process oriented organizations break down the barriers of structural departments and try to avoid functional silos.

    a. 33 Strategies of War
    b. Business process
    c. 1990 Clean Air Act
    d. 28-hour day

Chapter 3. Business Processes

4. _____ refers to the difference between the cost of materials purchased by a company plus the cost of the labor to assemble a product and the price at which the company sells the product. An example is the price of gasoline at the pump over the price of the oil in it. In national accounts used in macroeconomics, it refers to the contribution of the factors of production, i.e., land, labor, and capital goods, to raising the value of a product and corresponds to the incomes received by the owners of these factors.
    a. Rehn-Meidner Model
    b. Value added
    c. Minimum wage
    d. Deregulation

5. An _____ is typically a company that uses a component made by a second company in its own product or sells the product of the second company under its own brand. The specific meaning of the term varies in different contexts.
    a. AAAI
    b. Original equipment manufacturer
    c. A Stake in the Outcome
    d. A4e

6. A _____ is a common type of chart, that represents an algorithm or process, showing the steps as boxes of various kinds, and their order by connecting these with arrows. _____s are used in analyzing, designing, documenting or managing a process or program in various fields.

The first structured method for documenting process flow, the 'flow process chart', was introduced by Frank Gilbreth to members of ASME in 1921 as the presentation 'Process Charts--First Steps in Finding the One Best Way'.

    a. 1990 Clean Air Act
    b. 28-hour day
    c. 33 Strategies of War
    d. Flowchart

7. _____ is one of the four elements of marketing mix. An organization or set of organizations (go-betweens) involved in the process of making a product or service available for use or consumption by a consumer or business user.

The other three parts of the marketing mix are product, pricing, and promotion.

a. Matching theory
b. Job creation programs
c. Missing completely at random
d. Distribution

8. A _____ for a set of products is a warehouse or other specialized building, often with refrigeration or air conditioning, which is stocked with products (goods) to be re-distributed to retailers, wholesalers or directly to consumers. A _____ is a principle part, the 'order processing' element, of the entire 'order fulfillment' process. _____s are usually thought of as being 'demand driven'.
   a. Third-party logistics
   b. 1990 Clean Air Act
   c. 28-hour day
   d. Distribution center

9. In economics, business, retail, and accounting, a _____ is the value of money that has been used up to produce something, and hence is not available for use anymore. In economics, a _____ is an alternative that is given up as a result of a decision. In business, the _____ may be one of acquisition, in which case the amount of money expended to acquire it is counted as _____.
   a. Cost overrun
   b. Cost
   c. Cost allocation
   d. Fixed costs

10. _____ refers to metrics and measures of output from production processes, per unit of input. Labor _____, for example, is typically measured as a ratio of output per labor-hour, an input. _____ may be conceived of as a metrics of the technical or engineering efficiency of production.
    a. Master production schedule
    b. Productivity
    c. Value engineering
    d. Remanufacturing

11. _____ is one of the managerial functions like planning, organizing, staffing and directing. It is an important function because it helps to check the errors and to take the corrective action so that deviation from standards are minimized and stated goals of the organization are achieved in desired manner. According to modern concepts, _____ is a foreseeing action whereas earlier concept of _____ was used only when errors were detected. _____ in management means setting standards, measuring actual performance and taking corrective action.

Chapter 3. Business Processes

a. Turnover
b. Decision tree pruning
c. Schedule of reinforcement
d. Control

12. _____ is the process of comparing the cost, cycle time, productivity, or quality of a specific process or method to another that is widely considered to be an industry standard or best practice. Essentially, _____ provides a snapshot of the performance of your business and helps you understand where you are in relation to a particular standard. The result is often a business case for making changes in order to make improvements.

a. Complementors
b. Competitive heterogeneity
c. Benchmarking
d. Cost leadership

13. In probability theory, a probability distribution is called _____ if its cumulative distribution function is _____. This is equivalent to saying that for random variables X with the distribution in question, Pr[X = a] = 0 for all real numbers a, i.e.: the probability that X attains the value a is zero, for any number a. If the distribution of X is _____ then X is called a _____ random variable.

a. Pay Band
b. Connectionist expert systems
c. Continuous
d. Decision tree pruning

14. _____ is a management process whereby delivery (customer valued) processes are constantly evaluated and improved in the light of their efficiency, effectiveness and flexibility.

Some see it as a meta process for most management systems (Business Process Management, Quality Management, Project Management). Deming saw it as part of the 'system' whereby feedback from the process and customer were evaluated against organisational goals.

a. Sole proprietorship
b. Critical Success Factor
c. First-mover advantage
d. Continuous Improvement Process

Chapter 3. Business Processes

15. _____ is, in computer science and management, an approach aiming at improvements by means of elevating efficiency and effectiveness of the business process that exist within and across organizations. The key to _____ is for organizations to look at their business processes from a 'clean slate' perspective and determine how they can best construct these processes to improve how they conduct business. _____ Cycle.

_____ is also known as _____, Business Process Redesign, Business Transformation, or Business Process Change Management.

   a. Product life cycle
   b. Personal management interview
   c. Horizontal integration
   d. Business process reengineering

16. _____ is the process of understanding, anticipating and influencing consumer behavior in order to maximize revenue or profits from a fixed, perishable resource This process was first discovered by Dr. Matt H. Keller. The challenge is to sell the right resources to the right customer at the right time for the right price.
   a. Yield management
   b. Business model design
   c. Gap analysis
   d. Business networking

Chapter 4. Managing Quality

1. In probability theory, a probability distribution is called _____ if its cumulative distribution function is _____. This is equivalent to saying that for random variables X with the distribution in question, Pr[X = a] = 0 for all real numbers a, i.e.: the probability that X attains the value a is zero, for any number a. If the distribution of X is _____ then X is called a _____ random variable.

    a. Decision tree pruning
    b. Pay Band
    c. Connectionist expert systems
    d. Continuous

2. _____ is a management process whereby delivery (customer valued) processes are constantly evaluated and improved in the light of their efficiency, effectiveness and flexibility.

    Some see it as a meta process for most management systems (Business Process Management, Quality Management, Project Management). Deming saw it as part of the 'system' whereby feedback from the process and customer were evaluated against organisational goals.

    a. Continuous Improvement Process
    b. Critical Success Factor
    c. Sole proprietorship
    d. First-mover advantage

3. _____ is a business management strategy aimed at embedding awareness of quality in all organizational processes. _____ has been widely used in manufacturing, education, hospitals, call centers, government, and service industries, as well as NASA space and science programs.

    As defined by the International Organization for Standardization (ISO):

    '_____ is a management approach for an organization, centered on quality, based on the participation of all its members and aiming at long-term success through customer satisfaction, and benefits to all members of the organization and to society.' ISO 8402:1994

    One major aim is to reduce variation from every process so that greater consistency of effort is obtained. (Royse, D., Thyer, B., Padgett D., ' Logan T., 2006)

    a. Total quality management
    b. 1990 Clean Air Act
    c. Quality management
    d. 28-hour day

Chapter 4. Managing Quality

4. _____ is one of the managerial functions like planning, organizing, staffing and directing. It is an important function because it helps to check the errors and to take the corrective action so that deviation from standards are minimized and stated goals of the organization are achieved in desired manner. According to modern concepts, _____ is a foreseeing action whereas earlier concept of _____ was used only when errors were detected. _____ in management means setting standards, measuring actual performance and taking corrective action.
   a. Turnover
   b. Decision tree pruning
   c. Schedule of reinforcement
   d. Control

5. In engineering and manufacturing, _____ and quality engineering are used in developing systems to ensure products or services are designed and produced to meet or exceed customer requirements. Refer to the definition by Merriam-Webster for further information. These systems are often developed in conjunction with other business and engineering disciplines using a cross-functional approach.
   a. Process capability
   b. Single Minute Exchange of Die
   c. Statistical process control
   d. Quality control

6. _____ can be considered to have three main components: quality control, quality assurance and quality improvement. _____ is focused not only on product quality, but also the means to achieve it. _____ therefore uses quality assurance and control of processes as well as products to achieve more consistent quality.
   a. 1990 Clean Air Act
   b. 28-hour day
   c. Total quality management
   d. Quality management

7. In economics, and cost accounting, _____ describes the total economic cost of production and is made up of variable costs, which vary according to the quantity of a good produced and include inputs such as labor and raw materials, plus fixed costs, which are independent of the quantity of a good produced and include inputs (capital) that cannot be varied in the short term, such as buildings and machinery. _____ in economics includes the total opportunity cost of each factor of production in addition to fixed and variable costs.

The rate at which _____ changes as the amount produced changes is called marginal cost.

a. 1990 Clean Air Act
b. 28-hour day
c. 33 Strategies of War
d. Total cost

8. In economics, business, retail, and accounting, a _____ is the value of money that has been used up to produce something, and hence is not available for use anymore. In economics, a _____ is an alternative that is given up as a result of a decision. In business, the _____ may be one of acquisition, in which case the amount of money expended to acquire it is counted as _____.
   a. Cost
   b. Fixed costs
   c. Cost allocation
   d. Cost overrun

9. The concept of quality costs is a means to quantify the total _____-related efforts and deficiencies. It was first described by Armand V. Feigenbaum in a 1956 Harvard Business Review article.

Prior to its introduction, the general perception was that higher quality requires higher costs, either by buying better materials or machines or by hiring more labor.

   a. Fixed costs
   b. Quality costs
   c. Cost of Quality
   d. Cost accounting

10. _____ has been described as the 'process of social influence in which one person can enlist the aid and support of others in the accomplishment of a common task'. A definition more inclusive of followers comes from Alan Keith of Genentech who said '_____ is ultimately about creating a way for people to contribute to making something extraordinary happen.'

_____ is one of the most salient aspects of the organizational context. However, defining _____ has been challenging.

   a. 28-hour day
   b. 1990 Clean Air Act
   c. Situational leadership
   d. Leadership

Chapter 4. Managing Quality

11. _____ refers to increasing the spiritual, political, social or economic strength of individuals and communities. It often involves the empowered developing confidence in their own capacities.

The term Human _____ covers a vast landscape of meanings, interpretations, definitions and disciplines ranging from psychology and philosophy to the highly commercialized Self-Help industry and Motivational sciences.

a. A4e
b. AAAI
c. A Stake in the Outcome
d. Empowerment

12. _____ refers to planned and systematic production processes that provide confidence in a product's suitability for its intended purpose. Refer to the definition by Merriam-Webster for further information . It is a set of activities intended to ensure that products (goods and/or services) satisfy customer requirements in a systematic, reliable fashion.

a. Risk assessment
b. 28-hour day
c. 1990 Clean Air Act
d. Quality assurance

13. _____ is a 'method to transform user demands into design quality, to deploy the functions forming quality, and to deploy methods for achieving the design quality into subsystems and component parts, and ultimately to specific elements of the manufacturing process.' , as described by Dr. Yoji Akao, who originally developed _____ in Japan in 1966, when the author combined his work in quality assurance and quality control points with function deployment used in Value Engineering.

_____ is designed to help planners focus on characteristics of a new or existing product or service from the viewpoints of market segments, company, or technology-development needs. The technique yields graphs and matrices.

a. Learning organization
b. Quality function deployment
c. 1990 Clean Air Act
d. Hoshin Kanri

14. A _____ is a type of business entity in which partners (owners) share with each other the profits or losses of the business. _____s are often favored over corporations for taxation purposes, as the _____ structure does not generally incur a tax on profits before it is distributed to the partners (i.e. there is no dividend tax levied.) However, depending on the _____ structure and the jurisdiction in which it operates, owners of a _____ may be exposed to greater personal liability than they would as shareholders of a corporation.

Chapter 4. Managing Quality

a. Due process
b. Partnership
c. Mediation
d. Federal Employers Liability Act

15. _____ is a group creativity technique designed to generate a large number of ideas for the solution of a problem. The method was first popularized in the late 1930s by Alex Faickney Osborn in a book called Applied Imagination. Osborn proposed that groups could double their creative output with _____.

a. Adam Smith
b. Affiliation
c. Abraham Harold Maslow
d. Brainstorming

16. _____ ('Plan-Do-Check-Act') is an iterative four-step problem-solving process typically used in business process improvement. It is also known as the Deming Cycle, Shewhart cycle, Deming Wheel, or Plan-Do-Study-Act.

_____ was made popular by Dr. W. Edwards Deming, who is considered by many to be the father of modern quality control; however it was always referred to by him as the Shewhart cycle. Later in Deming's career, he modified _____ to Plan, Do, Study, Act (PDSA) so as to better describe his recommendations.

a. Management team
b. Decentralization
c. Management by exception
d. PDCA

17. _____ is a class of problem solving methods aimed at identifying the root causes of problems or events. The practice of _____ is predicated on the belief that problems are best solved by attempting to correct or eliminate root causes, as opposed to merely addressing the immediately obvious symptoms. By directing corrective measures at root causes, it is hoped that the likelihood of problem recurrence will be minimized.

a. 1990 Clean Air Act
b. Root cause analysis
c. Zero defects
d. 28-hour day

18. _____s are diagrams that show the causes of a certain event. A common use of the _____ is in product design, to identify potential factors causing an overall effect.

_____s were proposed by Kaoru Ishikawa in the 1960s, who pioneered quality management processes in the Kawasaki shipyards, and in the process became one of the founding fathers of modern management.

a. Ishikawa diagram
b. A4e
c. AAAI
d. A Stake in the Outcome

19. A _____ is a special type of bar chart where the values being plotted are arranged in descending order. The graph is accompanied by a line graph which shows the cumulative totals of each category, left to right. The chart was named for Vilfredo Pareto.

a. 33 Strategies of War
b. Pareto chart
c. 1990 Clean Air Act
d. 28-hour day

20. A _____ is a type of display using Cartesian coordinates to display values for two variables for a set of data.

The data is displayed as a collection of points, each having the value of one variable determining the position on the horizontal axis and the value of the other variable determining the position on the vertical axis. A _____ is also called a scatter chart, scatter diagram and scatter graph.

a. 33 Strategies of War
b. Scatter plot
c. 1990 Clean Air Act
d. 28-hour day

21. In statistics, a _____ is a graphical display of tabulated frequencies, shown as bars. It shows what proportion of cases fall into each of several categories: it is a form of data binning. The categories are usually specified as non-overlapping intervals of some variable.

a. Standard deviation
b. Statistics
c. Correlation
d. Histogram

22. A _____, also known as a run-sequence plot is a graph that displays observed data in a time sequence. Often, the data displayed represent some aspect of the output or performance of a manufacturing or other business process.

Run sequence plots are an easy way to graphically summarize a univariate data set.

a. 33 Strategies of War
b. 28-hour day
c. 1990 Clean Air Act
d. Run chart

23. The _____ is a measurable property of a process to the specification, expressed as a _____ index (e.g., C_{pk} or C_{pm}) or as a process performance index (e.g., P_{pk} or P_{pm}.) The output of this measurement is usually illustrated by a histogram and calculations that predict how many parts will be produced out of specification.

_____ is also defined as the capability of a process to meet its purpose as managed by an organization's management and process definition structures ISO 15504.

a. Single Minute Exchange of Die
b. Process capability
c. Statistical process control
d. Quality control

24. In process improvement efforts, the process capability index or _____ is a statistical measure of process capability: The ability of a process to produce output within engineering tolerances and specification limits. The concept of process capability only holds meaning for processes that are in a state of statistical control.

If the upper and lower specifications of the process are USL and LSL, the target process mean is T, the estimated mean of the process is $\hat{\mu}$ and the estimated variability of the process (expressed as a standard deviation) is $\hat{\sigma}$, then commonly-accepted process capability indices include:

$\hat{\sigma}$ is estimated using the sample standard deviation.

a. 1990 Clean Air Act
b. Process capability index
c. Constant dollars
d. Process capability ratio

Chapter 4. Managing Quality

25. Engineering _____ is the permissible limit of variation in

   1. a physical dimension,
   2. a measured value or physical property of a material, manufactured object, system, or service,
   3. other measured values (such as temperature, humidity, etc.)
   4. in engineering and safety, a physical distance or space (_____), as in a truck (lorry), train or boat under a bridge as well as a train in a tunnel

Dimensions, properties, or conditions may vary within certain practical limits without significantly affecting functioning of equipment or a process. _____s are specified to allow reasonable leeway for imperfections and inherent variability without compromising performance.

The _____ may be specified as a factor or percentage of the nominal value, a maximum deviation from a nominal value, an explicit range of allowed values, be specified by a note or published standard with this information, or be implied by the numeric accuracy of the nominal value. _____ can be symmetrical, as in 40±0.1, or asymmetrical, such as 40+0.2/−0.1.

   a. Zero defects
   b. Quality assurance
   c. Tolerance
   d. Root cause analysis

26. In process improvement efforts, the _____ or process capability ratio is a statistical measure of process capability: The ability of a process to produce output within engineering tolerances and specification limits. The concept of process capability only holds meaning for processes that are in a state of statistical control.

If the upper and lower specifications of the process are USL and LSL, the target process mean is T, the estimated mean of the process is $\hat{\mu}$ and the estimated variability of the process (expressed as a standard deviation) is $\hat{\sigma}$, then commonly-accepted process capability indices include:

$\hat{\sigma}$ is estimated using the sample standard deviation.

   a. 1990 Clean Air Act
   b. Process capability ratio
   c. Constant dollars
   d. Process capability index

27. The _____ in statistical process control is a tool used to determine whether a manufacturing or business process is in a state of statistical control or not.

Chapter 4. Managing Quality

If the chart indicates that the process is currently under control then it can be used with confidence to predict the future performance of the process. If the chart indicates that the process being monitored is not in control, the pattern it reveals can help determine the source of variation to be eliminated to bring the process back into control.

a. Time series analysis
b. Failure rate
c. Control chart
d. Simple moving average

28. _____ are horizontal lines drawn on an statistical process control chart, usually at a distance of >±3 standard deviations of the plotted statistic from the statistic's mean.

For normally distributed statistics, the area bracketed by the _____ will on average contain 99.73% of all the plot points on the chart, as long as the process is and remains in statistical control.

_____ should not be confused with tolerance limits, which are completely independent of the distribution of the plotted sample statistic.

a. 1990 Clean Air Act
b. Skewness risk
c. T-statistic
d. Control limits

29. An _____ is a specific member of a family of control charts. A control chart is a tool used in quality control, specifically SPC or statistical process control, as originally developed by Walter A. Shewhart at Western Electric in 1924 to improve the quality of telephones.

A control chart is a plot of measurements of a product on two special scales, usually located above and below each other and running horizontally. _____s consist of two charts, both with the same horizontal axis denoting the sample number.

a. 1990 Clean Air Act
b. 28-hour day
c. 33 Strategies of War
d. X-bar/R chart

30. In decision theory and estimation theory, the _____ of an estimator, $\hat{\theta}$, of an unknown parameter of the distribution, θ, is the expected value of the loss function

$$R(\theta, \hat{\theta}) = \mathbb{E}_\theta L(\theta, \hat{\theta}) = \int L(\theta, \hat{\theta})\, dP_\theta.$$

where dP_θ is a probability measure parametrized by θ.

- For a scalar parameter θ and a quadratic loss function,

$$L(\theta, \hat{\theta}) = (\theta - \hat{\theta})^2$$

the _____ function becomes the mean squared error of the estimate,

$$R(\theta, \hat{\theta}) = E_\theta(\theta - \hat{\theta})^2$$

- In density estimation, the unknown parameter is probability density itself. The loss function is typically chosen to be a norm in an appropriate function space. For example, for L^2 norm,

$$L(f, \hat{f}) = \|f - \hat{f}\|_2^2$$

the _____ function becomes the mean integrated squared error

$$R(f, \hat{f}) = E\|f - \hat{f}\|^2$$

a. Linear model
b. Risk aversion
c. Risk
d. Financial modeling

31. In statistics, decision theory and economics, a _____ is a function that maps an event (technically an element of a sample space) onto a real number representing the economic cost or regret associated with the event.

Less technically, in statistics a _____ represents the loss (cost in money or loss in utility in some other sense) associated with an estimate being 'wrong' (different from either a desired or a true value) as a function of a measure of the degree of wrongness (generally the difference between the estimated value and the true or desired value.)

Both Frequentist and Bayesian statistical theory involve calculating statistics in such a way as to minimize the expected loss observed from being wrong given a set of assumptions about the data and one's _____.

a. 1990 Clean Air Act
b. 33 Strategies of War
c. 28-hour day
d. Loss function

32. A _____ is the system of organizations, people, technology, activities, information and resources involved in moving a product or service from supplier to customer. _____ activities transform natural resources, raw materials and components into a finished product that is delivered to the end customer. In sophisticated _____ systems, used products may re-enter the _____ at any point where residual value is recyclable.

a. Wholesalers
b. Packaging
c. Drop shipping
d. Supply chain

33. _____ is a broad label that refers to any individuals or households that use goods and services generated within the economy. The concept of a _____ is used in different contexts, so that the usage and significance of the term may vary.

Typically when business people and economists talk of _____s they are talking about person as _____, an aggregated commodity item with little individuality other than that expressed in the buy/not-buy decision.

a. 1990 Clean Air Act
b. 33 Strategies of War
c. 28-hour day
d. Consumer

Chapter 5. Managing Projects

1. _____ refers to the movement of cash into or out of a business or financial product. It is usually measured during a specified, finite period of time. Measurement of _____ can be used

   - to determine a project's rate of return or value. The time of _____s into and out of projects are used as inputs in financial models such as internal rate of return, and net present value.
   - to determine problems with a business's liquidity. Being profitable does not necessarily mean being liquid. A company can fail because of a shortage of cash, even while profitable.
   - as an alternate measure of a business's profits when it is believed that accrual accounting concepts do not represent economic realities. For example, a company may be notionally profitable but generating little operational cash (as may be the case for a company that barters its products rather than selling for cash.) In such a case, the company may be deriving additional operating cash by issuing shares evaluating default risk, re-investment requirements, etc.

   _____ is a generic term used differently depending on the context. It may be defined by users for their own purposes.

   a. Cash flow
   b. Sweat equity
   c. Gross profit margin
   d. Gross profit

2. _____ is the discipline of planning, organizing and managing resources to bring about the successful completion of specific project goals and objectives. It is often closely related to and sometimes conflated with Program management.

   A project is a finite endeavor--having specific start and completion dates--undertaken to meet particular goals and objectives, usually to bring about beneficial change or added value.

   a. Work package
   b. Precedence diagram
   c. Project engineer
   d. Project management

3. A _____ is a type of bar chart that illustrates a project schedule. _____s illustrate the start and finish dates of the terminal elements and summary elements of a project. Terminal elements and summary elements comprise the work breakdown structure of the project.
   a. 33 Strategies of War
   b. 28-hour day
   c. 1990 Clean Air Act
   d. Gantt chart

4. The _____, is a mathematically based algorithm for scheduling a set of project activities. It is an important tool for effective project management.

Chapter 5. Managing Projects

It was developed in the 1950s by the Dupont Corporation at about the same time that General Dynamics and the US Navy were developing the Program Evaluation and Review Technique (PERT) Today, it is commonly used with all forms of projects, including construction, software development, research projects, product development, engineering, and plant maintenance, among others.

a. 28-hour day
b. Critical path method
c. 33 Strategies of War
d. 1990 Clean Air Act

5. The Program (or Project) Evaluation and Review Technique, commonly abbreviated _____, is a model for project management designed to analyze and represent the tasks involved in completing a given project.

_____ is a method to analyze the involved tasks in completing a given project, specially the time needed to complete each task, and identifying the minimum time needed to complete the total project.

_____ was developed primarily to simplify the planning and scheduling of large and complex projects.

a. 33 Strategies of War
b. PERT
c. 1990 Clean Air Act
d. 28-hour day

6. _____ is a company-wide computer software system used to manage and coordinate all the resources, information, and functions of a business from shared data stores.

An _____ system has a service-oriented architecture with modular hardware and software units and 'services' that communicate on a local area network. The modular design allows a business to add or reconfigure modules (perhaps from different vendors) while preserving data integrity in one shared database that may be centralized or distributed.

a. A Stake in the Outcome
b. A4e
c. AAAI
d. Enterprise resource planning

Chapter 6. Developing Products and Services

1. _____ is, in very basic words, a position a firm occupies against its competitors.

According to Michael Porter, the three methods for creating a sustainable _____ are through:

1. Cost leadership

2. Differentiation

3. Focus (economics)

  a. Theory Z
  b. Competitive advantage
  c. 1990 Clean Air Act
  d. 28-hour day

2. In economics, business, retail, and accounting, a _____ is the value of money that has been used up to produce something, and hence is not available for use anymore. In economics, a _____ is an alternative that is given up as a result of a decision. In business, the _____ may be one of acquisition, in which case the amount of money expended to acquire it is counted as _____.
  a. Cost
  b. Fixed costs
  c. Cost overrun
  d. Cost allocation

3. _____ is an advertisement in which a particular product specifically mentions a competitor by name for the express purpose of showing why the competitor is inferior to the product naming it.

This should not be confused with parody advertisements, where a fictional product is being advertised for the purpose of poking fun at the particular advertisement, nor should it be confused with the use of a coined brand name for the purpose of comparing the product without actually naming an actual competitor. ('Wikipedia tastes better and is less filling than the Encyclopedia Galactica.')

In the 1980s, during what has been referred to as the cola wars, soft-drink manufacturer Pepsi ran a series of advertisements where people, caught on hidden camera, in a blind taste test, chose Pepsi over rival Coca-Cola.

  a. 1990 Clean Air Act
  b. 33 Strategies of War
  c. Comparative advertising
  d. 28-hour day

Chapter 6. Developing Products and Services 33

4. In business and engineering, new _____ is the term used to describe the complete process of bringing a new product or service to market. There are two parallel paths involved in the NProduct development process: one involves the idea generation, product design, and detail engineering; the other involves market research and marketing analysis. Companies typically see new _____ as the first stage in generating and commercializing new products within the overall strategic process of product life cycle management used to maintain or grow their market share.
   a. 1990 Clean Air Act
   b. Product Development
   c. 33 Strategies of War
   d. 28-hour day

5. _____ is the variation in measurements taken by a single person or instrument on the same item and under the same conditions. A measurement may be said to be repeatable when this variation is smaller than some agreed limit. According to the Guidelines for Evaluating and Expressing the Uncertainty of NIST Measurement Results, _____ conditions include:

   - the same measurement procedure
   - the same observer
   - the same measuring instrument, used under the same conditions
   - the same location
   - repetition over a short period of time.

   _____ methods were developed by Bland and Altman (1986.) The _____ coefficient is a precision measure which represents the value below which the absolute difference between two repeated test results may be expected to lie with a probability of 95%.

   a. Spearman-Brown prediction formula
   b. Stanford-Binet Intelligence Scales
   c. Norm-referenced test
   d. Repeatability

6. _____ is something that a firm can do well and that meets the following three conditions:

Competencies are things that companys execute well across several business units or product sectors.

Firms usually have few competencies, but these are usually less liable to change rapidly.

   1. It provides consumer benefits
   2. It is not easy for competitors to imitate
   3. It can be leveraged widely to many products and markets.

A _____ can take various forms, including technical/subject matter know-how, a reliable process and/or close relationships with customers and suppliers (Mascarenhas et al. 1998.)

Chapter 6. Developing Products and Services

   a. Learning-by-doing
   b. NAIRU
   c. Dominant Design
   d. Core competency

7. A _____ is the system of organizations, people, technology, activities, information and resources involved in moving a product or service from supplier to customer. _____ activities transform natural resources, raw materials and components into a finished product that is delivered to the end customer. In sophisticated _____ systems, used products may re-enter the _____ at any point where residual value is recyclable.

   a. Supply chain
   b. Wholesalers
   c. Drop shipping
   d. Packaging

8. _____ is a work methodology based on the parallelization of tasks (ie. concurrently.) It refers to an approach used in product development in which functions of design engineering, manufacturing engineering and other functions are integrated to reduce the elapsed time required to bring a new product to the market.

   a. Concurrent engineering
   b. Work package
   c. Project management
   d. Critical Chain Project Management

9. _____ is an integrated communications-based process through which individuals and communities discover that existing and newly-identified needs and wants may be satisfied by the products and services of others.

_____ is defined by the American _____ Association as the activity, set of institutions, and processes for creating, communicating, delivering, and exchanging offerings that have value for customers, clients, partners, and society at large. The term developed from the original meaning which referred literally to going to market, as in shopping, or going to a market to buy or sell goods or services.

   a. Customer relationship management
   b. Disruptive technology
   c. Market development
   d. Marketing

Chapter 6. Developing Products and Services

10. _____ is a 'method to transform user demands into design quality, to deploy the functions forming quality, and to deploy methods for achieving the design quality into subsystems and component parts, and ultimately to specific elements of the manufacturing process.' , as described by Dr. Yoji Akao, who originally developed _____ in Japan in 1966, when the author combined his work in quality assurance and quality control points with function deployment used in Value Engineering.

_____ is designed to help planners focus on characteristics of a new or existing product or service from the viewpoints of market segments, company, or technology-development needs. The technique yields graphs and matrices.

a. Hoshin Kanri
b. 1990 Clean Air Act
c. Learning organization
d. Quality function deployment

11. _____ is a general concept that refers to a variety of design approaches that attempt to reduce the overall environmental impact of a product, process or service, where environmental impacts are considered across its life cycle.

Life cycle assessment (LCA) is employed to forecast the impacts of different (production) alternatives of the product in question, thus being able to choose the environmentally most friendly.

Different software tools have been developed to assist designers in finding optimized products (or processes/services.)

a. 28-hour day
b. Design methods
c. 1990 Clean Air Act
d. Design for environment

12. _____ is a pricing method used by firms. It is defined as 'a cost management tool for reducing the overall cost of a product over its entire life-cycle with the help of production, engineering, research and design'. A target cost is the maximum amount of cost that can be incurred on a product and with it the firm can still earn the required profit margin from that product at a particular selling price.
a. Pricing
b. Pricing objectives
c. Price war
d. Target costing

13.

_____ is a systematic method to improve the 'value' of goods or products and services by using an examination of function. Value, as defined, is the ratio of function to cost. Value can therefore be increased by either improving the function or reducing the cost.

a. Cellular manufacturing
b. Capacity planning
c. Master production schedule
d. Value engineering

Chapter 7. Process Choice and Layout Decisions in Manufacturing and Services

1. A _____ system is a manufacturing system in which there is some amount of flexibility that allows the system to react in the case of changes, whether predicted or unpredicted. This flexibility is generally considered to fall into two categories, which both contain numerous subcategories.

The first category, machine flexibility, covers the system's ability to be changed to produce new product types, and ability to change the order of operations executed on a part. The second category is called routing flexibility, which consists of the ability to use multiple machines to perform the same operation on a part, as well as the system's ability to absorb large-scale changes, such as in volume, capacity, or capability.

   a. Jidoka
   b. Manufacturing resource planning
   c. Homeworkers
   d. Flexible manufacturing

2. A _____ is a set of sequential operations established in a factory whereby materials are put through a refining process to produce an end-product that is suitable for onward consumption; or components are assembled to make a finished article.

Typically, raw materials such as metal ores or agricultural products such as foodstuffs or textile source plants (cotton, flax) require a sequence of treatments to render them useful. For metal, the processes include crushing, smelting and further refining.

   a. Production line
   b. Six Sigma
   c. Takt time
   d. Theory of constraints

3. In probability theory, a probability distribution is called _____ if its cumulative distribution function is _____. This is equivalent to saying that for random variables X with the distribution in question, Pr[X = a] = 0 for all real numbers a, i.e.: the probability that X attains the value a is zero, for any number a. If the distribution of X is _____ then X is called a _____ random variable.
   a. Connectionist expert systems
   b. Decision tree pruning
   c. Pay Band
   d. Continuous

4. _____ is a manufacturing strategy that produces a part via a just-in-time and kanban production approach, and calls for an ongoing examination and improvement efforts which ultimately requires integration of all elements of the production system. The goal is an optimally balanced production line with little waste, the lowest possible cost, on-time and defect-free production.

Chapter 7. Process Choice and Layout Decisions in Manufacturing and Services

This strategy is typically applied in discrete manufacturing as an attempt to handle production volumes comprising discrete units of product in a flow which is more naturally found in process manufacturing.

a. Quality control
b. Statistical process control
c. Process capability
d. Continuous flow manufacturing

5. _____ are typically small manufacturing operations that handle specialized manufacturing processes such as small customer orders or small batch jobs. _____ typically move on to different jobs (possibly with different customers) when each job is completed. By nature of this type of manufacturing operation, _____ are usually specialized in skill and processes.

a. 1990 Clean Air Act
b. Job shops
c. 28-hour day
d. 33 Strategies of War

6. A _____ is the system of organizations, people, technology, activities, information and resources involved in moving a product or service from supplier to customer. _____ activities transform natural resources, raw materials and components into a finished product that is delivered to the end customer. In sophisticated _____ systems, used products may re-enter the _____ at any point where residual value is recyclable.

a. Drop shipping
b. Wholesalers
c. Packaging
d. Supply chain

7. In economics, business, retail, and accounting, a _____ is the value of money that has been used up to produce something, and hence is not available for use anymore. In economics, a _____ is an alternative that is given up as a result of a decision. In business, the _____ may be one of acquisition, in which case the amount of money expended to acquire it is counted as _____.

a. Fixed costs
b. Cost overrun
c. Cost allocation
d. Cost

8. _____ in manufacturing refers to processes that occur later on in a production sequence or production line.

Chapter 7. Process Choice and Layout Decisions in Manufacturing and Services 39

Viewing a company 'from order to cash' might have high-level processes such as Marketing, Sales, Order Entry, Manufacturing, Packaging, Shipping, Invoicing. Each of these could be deconstructed into many sub-processes and supporting processes.

a. Science Learning Centre
b. Probability-generating function
c. Genbutsu
d. Downstream

9. _____ is an advertisement in which a particular product specifically mentions a competitor by name for the express purpose of showing why the competitor is inferior to the product naming it.

This should not be confused with parody advertisements, where a fictional product is being advertised for the purpose of poking fun at the particular advertisement, nor should it be confused with the use of a coined brand name for the purpose of comparing the product without actually naming an actual competitor. ('Wikipedia tastes better and is less filling than the Encyclopedia Galactica.')

In the 1980s, during what has been referred to as the cola wars, soft-drink manufacturer Pepsi ran a series of advertisements where people, caught on hidden camera, in a blind taste test, chose Pepsi over rival Coca-Cola.

a. 1990 Clean Air Act
b. 33 Strategies of War
c. 28-hour day
d. Comparative advertising

10. In marketing, _____ has come to mean the process by which marketers try to create an image or identity in the minds of their target market for its product, brand, or organization. It is the 'relative competitive comparison' their product occupies in a given market as perceived by the target market.

Re-_____ involves changing the identity of a product, relative to the identity of competing products, in the collective minds of the target market.

a. Positioning
b. PEST analysis
c. Context analysis
d. Customer analytics

Chapter 7. Process Choice and Layout Decisions in Manufacturing and Services

11. Appraisal is the third and last stage in using formal decision methods. The objective of the appraisal stage is for the decision maker to develop insight into the decision and determine a clear course of action. Much of the insight developed in this stage results from exploring the implications of the formal _____ developed during the formulation stage (i.e., from mining the model.)
    a. Decision Matrix
    b. Decision model
    c. Kepner-Tregoe
    d. Nominal group technique

12. _____ of the learning curve effect and the closely related experience curve effect express the relationship between equations for experience and efficiency or between efficiency gains and investment in the effort. The experience of 'learning curves' was first observed by the 19th Century German psychologist Hermann Ebbinghaus according to the difficulty of memorizing varying numbers of verbal stimuli, and subsequent learning about the complex processes of learning are discussed in the

The rule used for representing the learning curve effect states that the more times a task has been performed, the less time will be required on each subsequent iteration.

    a. Spatial Decision Support Systems
    b. Point biserial correlation coefficient
    c. Distribution
    d. Models

13. _____ can be defined as the maximum time per unit allowed to produce a product in order to meet demand. It is derived from the German word Taktzeit which translates to cycle time. _____ sets the pace for industrial manufacturing lines. In automobile manufacturing, for example, cars are assembled on a line, and are moved on to the next station after a certain time - the _____. Therefore, the time needed to complete work on each station has to be less than the _____ in order for the product to be completed within the alloted time.
    a. Six Sigma
    b. Theory of constraints
    c. Takt time
    d. Production line

14. A _____ is one scenario provided for evaluation by respondents in a Choice Experiment. Responses are collected and used to create a Choice Model. Respondents are usually provided with a series of differing _____s for evaluation.

a. Pairwise comparison
b. Choice Set
c. Computerized classification test
d. Thurstone scale

Chapter 8. Managing Capacity

1. _____ is an overall management philosophy introduced by Dr. Eliyahu M. Goldratt in his 1984 book titled The Goal, that is geared to help organizations continually achieve their goal. The title comes from the contention that any manageable system is limited in achieving more of its goal by a very small number of constraints, and that there is always at least one constraint. The _____ process seeks to identify the constraint and restructure the rest of the organization around it, through the use of the Five Focusing Steps.
   a. Takt time
   b. Production line
   c. Six Sigma
   d. Theory of Constraints

2. _____ is a Fortune 500, American multinational corporation headquartered in Cincinnati, Ohio, that manufactures a wide range of consumer goods. As of 2008, P'G is the 8th largest corporation in the world by market capitalization and 14th largest US company by profit.
   a. Turnover
   b. Maturity of Organizations and Business Excellence - The Four-Phase Model
   c. Procter ' Gamble Co.
   d. STAR

3. A _____ is the system of organizations, people, technology, activities, information and resources involved in moving a product or service from supplier to customer. _____ activities transform natural resources, raw materials and components into a finished product that is delivered to the end customer. In sophisticated _____ systems, used products may re-enter the _____ at any point where residual value is recyclable.
   a. Wholesalers
   b. Packaging
   c. Drop shipping
   d. Supply chain

4. In economics, business, retail, and accounting, a _____ is the value of money that has been used up to produce something, and hence is not available for use anymore. In economics, a _____ is an alternative that is given up as a result of a decision. In business, the _____ may be one of acquisition, in which case the amount of money expended to acquire it is counted as _____.
   a. Cost overrun
   b. Cost
   c. Fixed costs
   d. Cost allocation

5. In economics, _____ are business expenses that are not dependent on the activities of the business They tend to be time-related, such as salaries or rents being paid per month. This is in contrast to variable costs, which are volume-related (and are paid per quantity.)

In management accounting, _____ are defined as expenses that do not change in proportion to the activity of a business, within the relevant period or scale of production.

a. Cost allocation
b. Transaction cost
c. Cost of quality
d. Fixed costs

6. _____s are expenses that change in proportion to the activity of a business. In other words, _____ is the sum of marginal costs. It can also be considered normal costs.
a. Cost accounting
b. Variable cost
c. Cost overrun
d. Fixed costs

7. In economics, _____ is the desire to own something and the ability to pay for it. The term _____ signifies the ability or the willingness to buy a particular commodity at a given point of time.
a. 28-hour day
b. 1990 Clean Air Act
c. Demand
d. 33 Strategies of War

8. In probability theory and statistics, the _____ of a random variable is the integral of the random variable with respect to its probability measure. For discrete random variables this is equivalent to the probability-weighted sum of the possible values, and for continuous random variables with a density function it is the probability density-weighted integral of the possible values.
a. AAAI
b. A Stake in the Outcome
c. Expected value
d. A4e

9.

_____ is a systematic method to improve the 'value' of goods or products and services by using an examination of function. Value, as defined, is the ratio of function to cost. Value can therefore be increased by either improving the function or reducing the cost.

a. Master production schedule
b. Cellular manufacturing
c. Value engineering
d. Capacity planning

10. A _____ is a decision support tool that uses a tree-like graph or model of decisions and their possible consequences, including chance event outcomes, resource costs, and utility. _____s are commonly used in operations research, specifically in decision analysis, to help identify a strategy most likely to reach a goal. Another use of _____s is as a descriptive means for calculating conditional probabilities.
   a. 1990 Clean Air Act
   b. 28-hour day
   c. 33 Strategies of War
   d. Decision tree

11. _____ is one of the managerial functions like planning, organizing, staffing and directing. It is an important function because it helps to check the errors and to take the corrective action so that deviation from standards are minimized and stated goals of the organization are achieved in desired manner. According to modern concepts, _____ is a foreseeing action whereas earlier concept of _____ was used only when errors were detected. _____ in management means setting standards, measuring actual performance and taking corrective action.
   a. Decision tree pruning
   b. Schedule of reinforcement
   c. Turnover
   d. Control

12. The term _____ refers to a graphical representation of the 'average' rate of learning for an activity or tool. It can represent at a glance the initial difficulty of learning something and, to an extent, how much there is to learn after initial familiarity. For example, the Windows program Notepad is extremely simple to learn, but offers little after this.
   a. 1990 Clean Air Act
   b. 28-hour day
   c. 33 Strategies of War
   d. Learning curve

13. _____ is an advertisement in which a particular product specifically mentions a competitor by name for the express purpose of showing why the competitor is inferior to the product naming it.

Chapter 8. Managing Capacity

This should not be confused with parody advertisements, where a fictional product is being advertised for the purpose of poking fun at the particular advertisement, nor should it be confused with the use of a coined brand name for the purpose of comparing the product without actually naming an actual competitor. ('Wikipedia tastes better and is less filling than the Encyclopedia Galactica.')

In the 1980s, during what has been referred to as the cola wars, soft-drink manufacturer Pepsi ran a series of advertisements where people, caught on hidden camera, in a blind taste test, chose Pepsi over rival Coca-Cola.

a. 1990 Clean Air Act
b. 33 Strategies of War
c. 28-hour day
d. Comparative advertising

Chapter 9. Forecasting

1. _____ is the process of estimation in unknown situations. Prediction is a similar, but more general term. Both can refer to estimation of time series, cross-sectional or longitudinal data.
   a. 33 Strategies of War
   b. Forecasting
   c. 1990 Clean Air Act
   d. 28-hour day

2. _____ is a concept that aims to enhance supply chain integration by supporting and assisting joint practices. _____ seeks cooperative management of inventory through joint visibility and replenishment of products throughout the supply chain. Information shared between suppliers and retailers aids in planning and satisfying customer demands through a supportive system of shared information.
   a. Timesheets
   b. Collaborative Planning, Forecasting and Replenishment
   c. Groups decision making
   d. Career portfolios

3. In economics, _____ is the desire to own something and the ability to pay for it. The term _____ signifies the ability or the willingness to buy a particular commodity at a given point of time.
   a. 1990 Clean Air Act
   b. 33 Strategies of War
   c. 28-hour day
   d. Demand

4. _____ of the learning curve effect and the closely related experience curve effect express the relationship between equations for experience and efficiency or between efficiency gains and investment in the effort. The experience of 'learning curves' was first observed by the 19th Century German psychologist Hermann Ebbinghaus according to the difficulty of memorizing varying numbers of verbal stimuli, and subsequent learning about the complex processes of learning are discussed in the

.

The rule used for representing the learning curve effect states that the more times a task has been performed, the less time will be required on each subsequent iteration.

   a. Distribution
   b. Spatial Decision Support Systems
   c. Point biserial correlation coefficient
   d. Models

Chapter 9. Forecasting

5. The _____ is a systematic, interactive forecasting method which relies on a panel of independent experts. The carefully selected experts answer questionnaires in two or more rounds. After each round, a facilitator provides an anonymous summary of the experts' forecasts from the previous round as well as the reasons they provided for their judgments.

   a. Hoshin Kanri
   b. Learning organization
   c. Quality function deployment
   d. Delphi method

6. In statistics, signal processing, and many other fields, a _____ is a sequence of data points, measured typically at successive times, spaced at (often uniform) time intervals. _____ analysis comprises methods that attempt to understand such _____, often either to understand the underlying context of the data points (Where did they come from? What generated them?), or to make forecasts (predictions.) _____ forecasting is the use of a model to forecast future events based on known past events: to forecast future data points before they are measured.

   a. Time series
   b. Moving average
   c. Standard deviation
   d. Histogram

7. In statistics, many time series exhibit cyclic variation known as _____, periodic variation, or periodic fluctuations. This variation can be either regular or semiregular.

For example, retail sales tend to peak for the Christmas season and then decline after the holidays.

   a. 28-hour day
   b. 1990 Clean Air Act
   c. 33 Strategies of War
   d. Seasonality

8. The term '_____' refers to the concept of collecting information and attempting to spot a pattern in the information. In some fields of study, the term '_____' has more formally-defined meanings.

In project management _____ is a mathematical technique that uses historical results to predict future outcome.

a. Regression analysis
b. Stepwise regression
c. Least squares
d. Trend analysis

9. In statistics, a _____ rolling mean or running average, is a type of finite impulse response filter used to analyze a set of data points by creating a series of averages of different subsets of the full data set. A _____ is not a single number, but it is a set of numbers, each of which is the average of the corresponding subset of a larger set of data points. A _____ may also use unequal weights for each data value in the subset to emphasize particular values in the subset.
a. Time series analysis
b. Standard deviation
c. Homoscedastic
d. Moving average

10. In statistics and image processing, to smooth a data set is to create an approximating function that attempts to capture important patterns in the data, while leaving out noise or other fine-scale structures/rapid phenomena. Many different algorithms are used in _____. One of the most common algorithms is the 'moving average', often used to try to capture important trends in repeated statistical surveys.
a. 33 Strategies of War
b. Smoothing
c. 1990 Clean Air Act
d. 28-hour day

11. In statistics, _____ is a technique that can be applied to time series data, either to produce smoothed data for presentation, or to make forecasts. The time series data themselves are a sequence of observations. The observed phenomenon may be an essentially random process, or it may be an orderly, but noisy, process.
a. A Stake in the Outcome
b. Exponential smoothing
c. AAAI
d. A4e

12. In statistics, _____ is used for two things:

- to construct a simple formula that will predict a value or values for a variable given the value of another variable.
- to test whether and how a given variable is related to another variable or variables.

_____ is a form of regression analysis in which the relationship between one or more independent variables and another variable, called the dependent variable, is modelled by a least squares function, called a _____ equation. This function is a linear combination of one or more model parameters, called regression coefficients. A _____ equation with one independent variable represents a straight line when the predicted value (i.e. the dependent variable from the regression equation) is plotted against the independent variable: this is called a simple _____. However, note that 'linear' does not refer to this straight line, but rather to the way in which the regression coefficients occur in the regression equation.

a. Strict liability
b. Linear regression
c. Continuous
d. Clinical decision support systems

13. In statistics, _____ refers to techniques for the modeling and analysis of numerical data consisting of values of a dependent variable and of one or more independent variables The dependent variable in the regression equation is modeled as a function of the independent variables, corresponding parameters, and an error term. The error term is treated as a random variable and represents unexplained variation in the dependent variable.

a. Trend analysis
b. Least squares
c. Stepwise regression
d. Regression analysis

14. In the fields of science, engineering, industry and statistics, _____ is the degree of closeness of a measured or calculated quantity to its actual (true) value. _____ is closely related to precision, also called reproducibility or repeatability, the degree to which further measurements or calculations show the same or similar results. _____ indicates proximity to the true value, precision to the repeatability or reproducibility of the measurement

The results of calculations or a measurement can be accurate but not precise, precise but not accurate, neither, or both.

a. A4e
b. Accuracy
c. AAAI
d. A Stake in the Outcome

15. In statistics, _____ is:

- the arithmetic _____
- the expected value of a random variable, which is also called the population _____.

It is sometimes stated that the '_____' _____s average. This is incorrect if '_____' is taken in the specific sense of 'arithmetic _____' as there are different types of averages: the _____, median, and mode. Other simple statistical analyses use measures of spread, such as range, interquartile range, or standard deviation. For a real-valued random variable X, the _____ is the expectation of X. Note that not every probability distribution has a defined _____; see the Cauchy distribution for an example.

a. Correlation
b. Mean
c. Control chart
d. Statistical inference

16. The _____ or simply average deviation of a data set is the average of the absolute deviations and is a summary statistic of statistical dispersion or variability. It is also called the mean absolute deviation, but this is easily confused with the median absolute deviation.

The average absolute deviation of a set $\{x_1, x_2, ..., x_n\}$ is

The choice of measure of central tendency, m(X), has a marked effect on the value of the average deviation.

a. A Stake in the Outcome
b. A4e
c. Average absolute deviation,
d. AAAI

17. In statistics, a _____ is the difference between the actual or real and the predicted or forecast value of a time series or any other phenomenon of interest.

In simple cases, a forecast is compared with an outcome at a single time-point and a summary of _____s is constructed over a collection of such time-points. Here the forecast may be assessed using the difference or using a proportional error.

a. Forecast error
b. 1990 Clean Air Act
c. 33 Strategies of War
d. 28-hour day

18. _____ is a broad label that refers to any individuals or households that use goods and services generated within the economy. The concept of a _____ is used in different contexts, so that the usage and significance of the term may vary.

Typically when business people and economists talk of _____s they are talking about person as _____, an aggregated commodity item with little individuality other than that expressed in the buy/not-buy decision.

a. 1990 Clean Air Act
b. 33 Strategies of War
c. Consumer
d. 28-hour day

Chapter 10. Sourcing Decisions and the Purchasing Process

1. In business, the term word _____ refers to a number of procurement practices, aimed at finding, evaluating and engaging suppliers of goods and services:

   - Global _____, a procurement strategy aimed at exploiting global efficiencies in production
   - Strategic _____, a component of supply chain management, for improving and re-evaluating purchasing activities
   - _____, the identification of job candidates through proactive recruiting technique
   - Co-_____, a type of auditing service
   - Low-cost country _____, a procurement strategy for acquiring materials from countries with lower labour and production costs in order to cut operating expenses
   - Corporate _____, a supply chain, purchasing/procurement, and inventory function
   - Second-tier _____, a practice of rewarding suppliers for attempting to achieve minority-owned business spending goals of their customer
   - Netsourcing, a practice of utilizing an established group of businesses, individuals, or hardware ' software applications to streamline or initiate procurement practices by tapping in to and working through a third party provider
   - Inverted _____, a price volatility reduction strategy usually conducted by procurement or supply-chain person by which the value of an organization's waste-stream is maximized by actively seeking out the highest price possible from a range of potential buyers exploiting price trends and other market factors
   - Multisourcing, a strategy that treats a given function, such as IT, as a portfolio of activities, some of which should be outsourced and others of which should be performed by internal staff.
   - Crowdsourcing, using an undefined, generally large group of people or community in the form of an open call to perform a task

   In journalism, it can also refer to:

   - Journalism _____, the practice of identifying a person or publication that gives information
   - Single _____, the reuse of content in publishing

   In computing, it can refer to:

   - Open-_____, the act of releasing previously proprietary software under an open source/free software license
   - Power _____ equipment, network devices that will provide power in a Power over Ethernet (PoE) setup

   a. Cost Management
   b. Reinforcement
   c. Continuous
   d. Sourcing

2. A _____ is the system of organizations, people, technology, activities, information and resources involved in moving a product or service from supplier to customer. _____ activities transform natural resources, raw materials and components into a finished product that is delivered to the end customer. In sophisticated _____ systems, used products may re-enter the _____ at any point where residual value is recyclable.

Chapter 10. Sourcing Decisions and the Purchasing Process

a. Packaging
b. Supply chain
c. Wholesalers
d. Drop shipping

3. In economics, business, retail, and accounting, a _____ is the value of money that has been used up to produce something, and hence is not available for use anymore. In economics, a _____ is an alternative that is given up as a result of a decision. In business, the _____ may be one of acquisition, in which case the amount of money expended to acquire it is counted as _____.
   a. Cost
   b. Cost overrun
   c. Cost allocation
   d. Fixed costs

4. In financial accounting, _____ or cost of sales includes the direct costs attributable to the production of the goods sold by a company. This amount includes the materials cost used in creating the goods along with the direct labour costs used to produce the good. It excludes indirect expenses such as distribution costs and sales force costs.
   a. 28-hour day
   b. 1990 Clean Air Act
   c. Reorder point
   d. Cost of goods sold

5. _____, net margin, net _____ or net profit ratio all refer to a measure of profitability. It is calculated by finding the net profit as a percentage of the revenue.

$$\text{Net profit margin} = \frac{\text{Net profit (after taxes)}}{\text{Revenue}} \times 100\%$$

The _____ is mostly used for internal comparison.

   a. Net profit margin
   b. 1990 Clean Air Act
   c. Profit maximization
   d. Profit margin

6. The _____ percentage shows how profitable a company's assets are in generating revenue.

_____ can be computed as:

$$ROA = \frac{\text{Net Income} + \text{Interest Expense} - \text{Interest Tax savings}}{\text{Average Total Assets}}$$

This number tells you what the company can do with what it has, i.e. how many dollars of earnings they derive from each dollar of assets they control. Its a useful number for comparing competing companies in the same industry.

a. P/E ratio
b. Return on Capital Employed
c. Return on equity
d. Return on assets

7. In business and accounting, _____s are everything of value that is owned by a person or company. Any property or object of value that one possesses, usually considered as applicable to the payment of one's debts is considered an _____. Simplistically stated, _____s are things of value that can be readily converted into cash.

a. AAAI
b. A Stake in the Outcome
c. A4e
d. Asset

8. _____ is subcontracting a process, such as product design or manufacturing, to a third-party company. The decision to outsource is often made in the interest of lowering cost or making better use of time and energy costs, redirecting or conserving energy directed at the competencies of a particular business, or to make more efficient use of land, labor, capital, (information) technology and resources. _____ became part of the business lexicon during the 1980s.

a. Unemployment insurance
b. Opinion leadership
c. Operant conditioning
d. Outsourcing

9. _____ is something that a firm can do well and that meets the following three conditions:

Competencies are things that companys execute well across several business units or product sectors.

Chapter 10. Sourcing Decisions and the Purchasing Process

Firms usually have few competencies, but these are usually less liable to change rapidly.

1. It provides consumer benefits
2. It is not easy for competitors to imitate
3. It can be leveraged widely to many products and markets.

A _____ can take various forms, including technical/subject matter know-how, a reliable process and/or close relationships with customers and suppliers (Mascarenhas et al. 1998.)

a. NAIRU
b. Learning-by-doing
c. Dominant Design
d. Core competency

10. In economics, and cost accounting, _____ describes the total economic cost of production and is made up of variable costs, which vary according to the quantity of a good produced and include inputs such as labor and raw materials, plus fixed costs, which are independent of the quantity of a good produced and include inputs (capital) that cannot be varied in the short term, such as buildings and machinery. _____ in economics includes the total opportunity cost of each factor of production in addition to fixed and variable costs.

The rate at which _____ changes as the amount produced changes is called marginal cost.

a. 28-hour day
b. 1990 Clean Air Act
c. 33 Strategies of War
d. Total cost

11. _____ are costs that are not directly accountable to a particular function or product. _____ may be either fixed or variable. _____ include taxes, administration, personnel and security costs, and are also known as overhead.

a. Activity-based management
b. A Stake in the Outcome
c. A4e
d. Indirect costs

12.

The _____ can vary from one organization to another but there are some key elements that are common throughout

Chapter 10. Sourcing Decisions and the Purchasing Process

The process usually starts with a 'Demand' or requirements - this could be for a physical part (inventory) or a service. A requisition is generated, which details the requirements (in some cases providing a requirements speciation) which actions the procurement department. An RFP or RFQ is then raised (request for proposal or Request for quotation.)

a. 1990 Clean Air Act
b. Purchasing process
c. Purchase requisition
d. Request for quotation

13. As part of an organization's internal financial controls, the accounting department may institute a _____ process to help manage requests for purchases. Requests for the creation of purchase of goods and services are documented and routed for approval within the organization and then delivered to the accounting group.

Typically an accounting staff member is assigned responsibility for purchase order management, referred to commonly as the PO (purchase order) Coordinator.

a. Request for quotation
b. 1990 Clean Air Act
c. Purchasing process
d. Purchase requisition

14. The _____ is the level of inventory when a fresh order should be made with suppliers to bring the inventory up by the Economic order quantity ('EOQ'.)

The _____ for replenishment of stock occurs when the level of inventory drops down to zero. In view of instantaneous replenishment of stock the level of inventory jumps to the original level from zero level.

a. 1990 Clean Air Act
b. 28-hour day
c. Finished goods
d. Reorder point

15. A _____ is a name or trademark connected with a product or producer. _____s have become increasingly important components of culture and the economy, now being described as 'cultural accessories and personal philosophies'.

Some people distinguish the psychological aspect of a _____ from the experiential aspect.

a. Brand awareness
b. Brand loyalty
c. Brand extension
d. Brand

16. _____, headquartered in Short Hills, New Jersey, USA, is a provider of credit information on businesses and corporations. Often referred to as just D'B, the company is perhaps best known for its D-U-N-S (Data Universal Numbering System) identifiers assigned to over 100 million global companies.

D'B's D-U-N-S Numbers are Business Information Reports.

a. Prometric
b. Sears Holdings Corporation
c. PeopleSoft, Inc.
d. The Dun ' Bradstreet Corporation

17. _____ is one of the managerial functions like planning, organizing, staffing and directing. It is an important function because it helps to check the errors and to take the corrective action so that deviation from standards are minimized and stated goals of the organization are achieved in desired manner. According to modern concepts, _____ is a foreseeing action whereas earlier concept of _____ was used only when errors were detected. _____ in management means setting standards, measuring actual performance and taking corrective action.

a. Control
b. Decision tree pruning
c. Schedule of reinforcement
d. Turnover

18. _____ is the acquisition of goods and/or services at the best possible total cost of ownership, in the right quality and quantity, at the right time, in the right place and from the right source for the direct benefit or use of corporations, individuals generally via a contract. Simple _____ may involve nothing more than repeat purchasing. Complex _____ could involve finding long term partners - or even 'co-destiny' suppliers that might fundamentally commit one organization to another.

a. Golden parachute
b. Psychological pricing
c. Procurement
d. Sole proprietorship

Chapter 10. Sourcing Decisions and the Purchasing Process

19. _____ is a Fortune 500, American multinational corporation headquartered in Cincinnati, Ohio, that manufactures a wide range of consumer goods. As of 2008, P'G is the 8th largest corporation in the world by market capitalization and 14th largest US company by profit.
   a. STAR
   b. Turnover
   c. Maturity of Organizations and Business Excellence - The Four-Phase Model
   d. Procter ' Gamble Co.

20. _____ refers to the structured transmission of data between organizations by electronic means. It is used to transfer electronic documents from one computer system to another (ie) from one trading partner to another trading partner. It is more than mere E-mail; for instance, organizations might replace bills of lading and even checks with appropriate _____ messages.
   a. A4e
   b. Electronic data interchange
   c. AAAI
   d. A Stake in the Outcome

21. A _____ is a commercial document issued by a buyer to a seller, indicating types, quantities, and agreed prices for products or services the seller will provide to the buyer. Sending a _____ to a supplier constitutes a legal offer to buy products or services. Acceptance of a _____ by a seller usually forms a one-off contract between the buyer and seller, so no contract exists until the _____ is accepted.
   a. 28-hour day
   b. 1990 Clean Air Act
   c. 33 Strategies of War
   d. Purchase order

22. A _____ is a standard business process whose purpose is to invite suppliers into a bidding process to bid on specific products or services.

An _____ typically involves more than the price per item. Information like payment terms, quality level per item or contract length are possible to be requested during the bidding process.

   a. 1990 Clean Air Act
   b. Request for quotation
   c. Purchasing process
   d. Purchase requisition

Chapter 10. Sourcing Decisions and the Purchasing Process

23. A _____ is a document that captures and agrees the work activities, deliverables and timeline that a vendor will execute against in performance of work for a customer. Detailed requirements and pricing are usually specified in a _____, along with many other terms and conditions.

There are many formats and styles of _____ document templates that have been specialized for the Hardware or Software solutions being described in the Request for Proposal.

   a. 1990 Clean Air Act
   b. 28-hour day
   c. Statement of work
   d. Modular design

24. The _____ is a structured technique for dealing with complex decisions. Rather than prescribing a 'correct' decision, the _____ helps the decision makers find the one that best suits their needs and their understanding of the problem.

Based on mathematics and psychology, it was developed by Thomas L. Saaty in the 1970s and has been extensively studied and refined since then.

   a. Analytic hierarchy process
   b. A4e
   c. A Stake in the Outcome
   d. AAAI

25. Appraisal is the third and last stage in using formal decision methods. The objective of the appraisal stage is for the decision maker to develop insight into the decision and determine a clear course of action. Much of the insight developed in this stage results from exploring the implications of the formal _____ developed during the formulation stage (i.e., from mining the model.)
   a. Decision model
   b. Nominal group technique
   c. Decision Matrix
   d. Kepner-Tregoe

26. _____ of the learning curve effect and the closely related experience curve effect express the relationship between equations for experience and efficiency or between efficiency gains and investment in the effort. The experience of 'learning curves' was first observed by the 19th Century German psychologist Hermann Ebbinghaus according to the difficulty of memorizing varying numbers of verbal stimuli, and subsequent learning about the complex processes of learning are discussed in the

Chapter 10. Sourcing Decisions and the Purchasing Process

The rule used for representing the learning curve effect states that the more times a task has been performed, the less time will be required on each subsequent iteration.

a. Point biserial correlation coefficient
b. Distribution
c. Spatial Decision Support Systems
d. Models

27. The term '_____' refers to the concept of collecting information and attempting to spot a pattern in the information. In some fields of study, the term '_____' has more formally-defined meanings.

In project management _____ is a mathematical technique that uses historical results to predict future outcome.

a. Least squares
b. Regression analysis
c. Trend analysis
d. Stepwise regression

28. _____ describes commerce transactions between businesses, such as between a manufacturer and a wholesaler, or between a wholesaler and a retailer. Contrasting terms are business-to-consumer (B2C) and business-to-government (B2G).

The volume of B2B transactions is much higher than the volume of B2C transactions.

a. Product bundling
b. Market environment
c. Category management
d. Business-to-business

29. _____ is the process whereby an organization establishes the parameters within which programs, investments, and acquisitions are reaching the desired results. Performance Reference Model of the Federal Enterprise Architecture, 2005.

This process of measuring performance often requires the use of statistical evidence to determine progress toward specific defined organizational objectives.

There are many types of measurements.

a. Workflow
b. CIFMS
c. Crisis management
d. Performance measurement

30. The _____ is a not-for-profit United States association for the benefit of the purchasing and supply management profession, particularly in the areas of education and research.

It was founded in 1913 as the New York Association of Purchasing Management after a purchasing meeting organized by the Thomas Register. It was established in 1915 as the National Association of Purchasing Management.

a. A4e
b. AAAI
c. A Stake in the Outcome
d. Institute for Supply Management

31. _____ is the management of purchasing process, and related aspects in an organization. Because of production companies purchase nowadays about 70% of their turnover, and service companies purchase approximately 40% of their turnover, _____ is one of the most critical areas in the entire organization and needs intensive management.

Purchasing Process includes as usual 8 main stages as follows:

1. Requisitioning
2. Approving
3. Studying Market
4. Making Purchase Decision
5. Placing Orders
6. Receipting Goods and Services Received
7. Accounting Goods and Services
8. Receiving Invoices and Making Payment
9. Debit note in case of material defect

_____ Process consists usually of 3 stages:

1. Purchasing Planning
2. Purchasing Tracking
3. Purchasing Reporting

Chapter 10. Sourcing Decisions and the Purchasing Process

Purchasing Planning may include steps as follows:

- creating purchasing projects and tasks
- providing related information (files, links, notes etc.)
- assigning purchasing tasks to employees
- setting task priorities, start/finish dates etc.
- assigning supervisors
- setting reminders

Purchasing Tracking consists of:

- checking task's status and/or history of changes
- receiving status notifications
- sorting, grouping or filtering tasks by current status
- highlighting overdue tasks

Purchasing Reporting includes:

- comparing actual and estimated values
- calculating purchasing task and project statistics
- sorting, grouping or filtering tasks by attributes
- creating charts to visualize key statistics and KPIs

a. Catfish effect
b. Cross ownership
c. Getting Things Done
d. Purchasing Management

32. _____-model (SCOR(r)) is a process reference model developed by the management consulting firm PRTM and AMR Research and endorsed by the Supply-Chain Council (SCC) as the cross-industry de facto standard diagnostic tool for supply chain management. SCOR enables users to address, improve, and communicate supply chain management practices within and between all interested parties in the Extended Enterprise.

SCOR(r) is a management tool, spanning from the supplier's supplier to the customer's customer. The model has been developed by the members of the Council on a volunteer basis to describe the business activities associated with all phases of satisfying a customer's demand.

a. Supply Chain Risk Management
b. Supply-Chain Operations Reference
c. Supply chain management software
d. Delayed differentiation

Chapter 11. Logistics

1. _____ is the management of the flow of goods, information and other resources, including energy and people, between the point of origin and the point of consumption in order to meet the requirements of consumers (frequently, and originally, military organizations.) _____ involves the integration of information, transportation, inventory, warehousing, material-handling, and packaging, and occasionally security. _____ is a channel of the supply chain which adds the value of time and place utility.

   a. 28-hour day
   b. 1990 Clean Air Act
   c. Third-party logistics
   d. Logistics

2. The _____ of 1980, signed into law by President Jimmy Carter on October 14, deregulated the railroad industry (to a significant extent) and replaced the regulatory structure that existed since the 1887 Interstate Commerce Act.

   This Act followed the Railroad Revitalization and Regulatory Reform Act of 1976, which established the basic outlines of regulatory reform in the railroad industry -- greater range for railroad pricing without close regulatory restraint, greater independence from collective rate making procedures in rail pricing and service offers, contract rates, and, to a lesser extent, greater freedom for entry into and exit from rail markets.

   Though the '4R' Act established these guidelines, the Interstate Commerce Commission at first did not give much effect to its legislative mandates.

   a. 28-hour day
   b. 33 Strategies of War
   c. 1990 Clean Air Act
   d. Staggers Rail Act

3. _____ is the removal or simplification of government rules and regulations that constrain the operation of market forces. _____ does not mean elimination of laws against fraud, but eliminating or reducing government control of how business is done, thereby moving toward a more free market.

   The stated rationale for '_____' is often that fewer and simpler regulations will lead to a raised level of competitiveness, therefore higher productivity, more efficiency and lower prices overall.

   a. Natural rate of unemployment
   b. Value added
   c. Rehn-Meidner Model
   d. Deregulation

4. _____ in its literal sense is the process of transformation of local or regional phenomena into global ones. It can be described as a process by which the people of the world are unified into a single society and function together.

This process is a combination of economic, technological, sociocultural and political forces.

a. Cost Management
b. Histogram
c. Collaborative Planning, Forecasting and Replenishment
d. Globalization

5. _____ is an advertisement in which a particular product specifically mentions a competitor by name for the express purpose of showing why the competitor is inferior to the product naming it.

This should not be confused with parody advertisements, where a fictional product is being advertised for the purpose of poking fun at the particular advertisement, nor should it be confused with the use of a coined brand name for the purpose of comparing the product without actually naming an actual competitor. ('Wikipedia tastes better and is less filling than the Encyclopedia Galactica.')

In the 1980s, during what has been referred to as the cola wars, soft-drink manufacturer Pepsi ran a series of advertisements where people, caught on hidden camera, in a blind taste test, chose Pepsi over rival Coca-Cola.

a. 28-hour day
b. Comparative advertising
c. 33 Strategies of War
d. 1990 Clean Air Act

6. _____ is an integrated business management process through which the executive/leadership team continually achieves focus, alignment and synchronization among all the functions of the organization. The monthly S'OP plan includes an updated sales plan, production plan, inventory plan, customer lead time (backlog) plan, new product development plan, strategic initiative plan and resulting financial plan. Done well, the S'OP process also enables effective supply chain management.

a. 1990 Clean Air Act
b. 28-hour day
c. 33 Strategies of War
d. Sales and operations planning

7. A _____ is a commercial building for storage of goods. _____s are used by manufacturers, importers, exporters, wholesalers, transport businesses, customs, etc. They are usually large plain buildings in industrial areas of cities and towns.

a. 33 Strategies of War
b. 28-hour day
c. 1990 Clean Air Act
d. Warehouse

8. _____ is a practice in logistics of unloading materials from an incoming semi-trailer truck or rail car and loading these materials directly into outbound trucks, trailers with little or no storage in between. This may be done to change type of conveyance, to sort material intended for different destinations or similar destination.

Cross-Dock operations were first pioneered in the US trucking industry in the 1930's, and have been in continuous use in LTL (less than truckload) operations ever since.

a. Small business
b. Cross-docking
c. Corporate recovery
d. Product life cycle

9. _____ or Postponement is a concept in supply chain management where the manufacturing process starts by making a generic or family product that is later differentiated into a specific end-product. This is a widely used method, especially in industries with high demand uncertainty, and can be effectively used to address the final demand even if forecasts cannot be improved.

An example would be Benetton and their knitted sweaters that are initially all white, and then dyed into different colors only when the season/customer color preference/demand is known.

a. Materials management
b. Delayed differentiation
c. Supply-Chain Operations Reference
d. Demand chain

10. A _____ is the period of time between the initiation of any process of production and the completion of that process. Thus the _____ for ordering a new car from a manufacturer may be anywhere from 2 weeks to 6 months. In industry, _____ reduction is an important part of lean manufacturing.

a. 33 Strategies of War
b. 28-hour day
c. 1990 Clean Air Act
d. Lead time

Chapter 11. Logistics

11. _____ is a term used by inventory specialists to describe a level of extra stock that is maintained below the cycle stock to buffer against stockouts. _____ exists to counter uncertainties in supply and demand. _____ is defined as extra units of inventory carried as protection against possible stockouts .(shortfall in raw material or packaging.)
   a. Knowledge worker
   b. Process automation
   c. Product life cycle
   d. Safety stock

12. _____ is the science, art and technology of enclosing or protecting products for distribution, storage, sale, and use. _____ also refers to the process of design, evaluation, and production of packages. _____ can be described as a coordinated system of preparing goods for transport, warehousing, logistics, sale, and end use.
   a. Supply chain management
   b. Wholesalers
   c. Supply chain
   d. Packaging

13. _____ is subcontracting a process, such as product design or manufacturing, to a third-party company. The decision to outsource is often made in the interest of lowering cost or making better use of time and energy costs, redirecting or conserving energy directed at the competencies of a particular business, or to make more efficient use of land, labor, capital, (information) technology and resources. _____ became part of the business lexicon during the 1980s.
   a. Operant conditioning
   b. Opinion leadership
   c. Outsourcing
   d. Unemployment insurance

14. _____ is a profession that involves the 'clearing' of goods through customs barriers for importers and exporters (usually businesses.) This involves the preparation of documents and/or electronic submissions, the calculation (and usually the payment) on behalf of the client of taxes, duties and excises, and facilitating communication between the importer/exporter and governmental authorities. Customs brokers in the USA will often prepare and submit documentation to notify or obtain the clearance from other government agencies such as the Food and Drug Administration (FDA), the United States Department of Agriculture (USDA), the Fish and Wildlife Service, and many others.
   a. Customs brokerage
   b. Trade creation
   c. Trade barrier
   d. Most favoured nation

Chapter 11. Logistics

15. A _____ is a third party logistics provider. As a third party (or non asset based) provider a forwarder dispatches shipments via asset-based carriers and books or otherwise arranges space for those shipments. Carrier types include waterborne vessels, airplanes, trucks or railroads.
    a. Supply chain management
    b. Freight forwarder
    c. Drop shipping
    d. Supply chain

16. There are many important decisions about product and service development and marketing. In the process of product development and marketing we should focus on strategic decisions about product attributes, product branding, product packaging, product labeling and product support services. But product strategy also calls for building a _____.
    a. Product Line
    b. Marketing strategy
    c. Product bundling
    d. Context analysis

17. In economics, business, retail, and accounting, a _____ is the value of money that has been used up to produce something, and hence is not available for use anymore. In economics, a _____ is an alternative that is given up as a result of a decision. In business, the _____ may be one of acquisition, in which case the amount of money expended to acquire it is counted as _____.
    a. Fixed costs
    b. Cost overrun
    c. Cost allocation
    d. Cost

18. Appraisal is the third and last stage in using formal decision methods. The objective of the appraisal stage is for the decision maker to develop insight into the decision and determine a clear course of action. Much of the insight developed in this stage results from exploring the implications of the formal _____ developed during the formulation stage (i.e., from mining the model.)
    a. Decision model
    b. Nominal group technique
    c. Kepner-Tregoe
    d. Decision Matrix

Chapter 11. Logistics

19. _____ of the learning curve effect and the closely related experience curve effect express the relationship between equations for experience and efficiency or between efficiency gains and investment in the effort. The experience of 'learning curves' was first observed by the 19th Century German psychologist Hermann Ebbinghaus according to the difficulty of memorizing varying numbers of verbal stimuli, and subsequent learning about the complex processes of learning are discussed in the

.

The rule used for representing the learning curve effect states that the more times a task has been performed, the less time will be required on each subsequent iteration.

a. Models
b. Distribution
c. Spatial Decision Support Systems
d. Point biserial correlation coefficient

20. The _____ is one of the fundamental combinatorial optimization problems in the branch of optimization or operations research in mathematics. It consists of finding a maximum weight matching in a weighted bipartite graph.

In its most general form, the problem is as follows:

There are a number of agents and a number of tasks.

a. A Stake in the Outcome
b. Assignment problem
c. AAAI
d. A4e

21. The function f is called, variously, an _____, cost function, energy function, or energy functional. A feasible solution that minimizes (or maximizes, if that is the goal) the _____ is called an optimal solution.

Generally, when the feasible region or the _____ of the problem does not present convexity, there may be several local minima and maxima, where a local minimum x^* is defined as a point for which there exists some $>\delta > 0$ so that for all x such that

$\boxed{x}$ >

the expression

$$f(x^*) \geq$$

holds; that is to say, on some region around x* all of the function values are greater than or equal to the value at that point.

a. A Stake in the Outcome
b. Objective function
c. A4e
d. AAAI

22. _____ is an inventory strategy that strives to improve the return on investment of a business by reducing in-process inventory and its associated carrying costs. To meet _____ objectives, the process relies on signals between different points in the process. This means the process is often driven by a series of signals, or Kanban , which tell production when to make the next part. Kanban are usually 'tickets' but can be simple visual signals, such as the presence or absence of a part on a shelf. Implemented correctly, _____ can dramatically improve a manufacturing organization's return on investment, quality, and efficiency.
a. 28-hour day
b. 33 Strategies of War
c. 1990 Clean Air Act
d. Just-in-time

Chapter 12. Sales and Operations Planning (Aggregate Planning)

1. _____ is an operational activity which does an aggregate plan for the production process, in advance of 2 to 18 months, to give an idea to management as to what quantity of materials and other resources are to be procured and when, so that the total cost of operations of the organization is kept to the minimum over that period.

The quantity of outsourcing, subcontracting of items, overtime of labor, numbers to be hired and fired in each period and the amount of inventory to be held in stock and to be backlogged for each period are decided. All of these activities are done within the framework of the company ethics, policies, and long term commitment to the society, community and the country of operation.

   a. Earned Schedule
   b. Aggregate planning
   c. A Stake in the Outcome
   d. Earned value management

2. _____ is an integrated business management process through which the executive/leadership team continually achieves focus, alignment and synchronization among all the functions of the organization. The monthly S'OP plan includes an updated sales plan, production plan, inventory plan, customer lead time (backlog) plan, new product development plan, strategic initiative plan and resulting financial plan. Done well, the S'OP process also enables effective supply chain management.

   a. 28-hour day
   b. Sales and operations planning
   c. 33 Strategies of War
   d. 1990 Clean Air Act

3. _____ is an organization's process of defining its strategy and making decisions on allocating its resources to pursue this strategy, including its capital and people. Various business analysis techniques can be used in _____, including SWOT analysis (Strengths, Weaknesses, Opportunities, and Threats) and PEST analysis (Political, Economic, Social, and Technological analysis) or STEER analysis involving Socio-cultural, Technological, Economic, Ecological, and Regulatory factors and EPISTEL (Environment, Political, Informatic, Social, Technological, Economic and Legal)

_____ is the formal consideration of an organization's future course. All _____ deals with at least one of three key questions:

   1. 'What do we do?'
   2. 'For whom do we do it?'
   3. 'How do we excel?'

In business _____, the third question is better phrased 'How can we beat or avoid competition?'. (Bradford and Duncan, page 1.)

Chapter 12. Sales and Operations Planning (Aggregate Planning)

a. 33 Strategies of War
b. 28-hour day
c. Strategic planning
d. 1990 Clean Air Act

4. _____ is one of the managerial functions like planning, organizing, staffing and directing. It is an important function because it helps to check the errors and to take the corrective action so that deviation from standards are minimized and stated goals of the organization are achieved in desired manner. According to modern concepts, _____ is a foreseeing action whereas earlier concept of _____ was used only when errors were detected. _____ in management means setting standards, measuring actual performance and taking corrective action.

a. Schedule of reinforcement
b. Turnover
c. Control
d. Decision tree pruning

5. _____ refers to the movement of cash into or out of a business or financial product. It is usually measured during a specified, finite period of time. Measurement of _____ can be used

- to determine a project's rate of return or value. The time of _____s into and out of projects are used as inputs in financial models such as internal rate of return, and net present value.
- to determine problems with a business's liquidity. Being profitable does not necessarily mean being liquid. A company can fail because of a shortage of cash, even while profitable.
- as an alternate measure of a business's profits when it is believed that accrual accounting concepts do not represent economic realities. For example, a company may be notionally profitable but generating little operational cash (as may be the case for a company that barters its products rather than selling for cash.) In such a case, the company may be deriving additional operating cash by issuing shares evaluating default risk, re-investment requirements, etc.

_____ is a generic term used differently depending on the context. It may be defined by users for their own purposes.

a. Sweat equity
b. Gross profit margin
c. Gross profit
d. Cash flow

6. _____ is the provision of service to customers before, during and after a purchase.

According to Turban et al. (2002), '_____ is a series of activities designed to enhance the level of customer satisfaction - that is, the feeling that a product or service has met the customer expectation.'

Chapter 12. Sales and Operations Planning (Aggregate Planning)

Its importance varies by product, industry and customer; defective or broken merchandise can be exchanged, often only with a receipt and within a specified time frame.

a. Service rate
b. 1990 Clean Air Act
c. 28-hour day
d. Customer service

7. _____ is an advertisement in which a particular product specifically mentions a competitor by name for the express purpose of showing why the competitor is inferior to the product naming it.

This should not be confused with parody advertisements, where a fictional product is being advertised for the purpose of poking fun at the particular advertisement, nor should it be confused with the use of a coined brand name for the purpose of comparing the product without actually naming an actual competitor. ('Wikipedia tastes better and is less filling than the Encyclopedia Galactica.')

In the 1980s, during what has been referred to as the cola wars, soft-drink manufacturer Pepsi ran a series of advertisements where people, caught on hidden camera, in a blind taste test, chose Pepsi over rival Coca-Cola.

a. 33 Strategies of War
b. Comparative advertising
c. 1990 Clean Air Act
d. 28-hour day

8. The _____ is the amount of time an organization will look into the future when preparing a strategic plan. Many commercial companies use a five-year _____, but other organizations such as the Forestry Commission in the UK have to use a much longer _____ to form effective plans.

a. Strategic Alliance
b. Planning horizon
c. No-bid contract
d. Psychological pricing

9. _____ is, in very basic words, a position a firm occupies against its competitors.

According to Michael Porter, the three methods for creating a sustainable _____ are through:

1. Cost leadership

Chapter 12. Sales and Operations Planning (Aggregate Planning)

2. Differentiation

3. Focus (economics)

   a. Competitive advantage
   b. 28-hour day
   c. Theory Z
   d. 1990 Clean Air Act

10. In probability theory, a probability distribution is called _____ if its cumulative distribution function is _____. This is equivalent to saying that for random variables X with the distribution in question, Pr[X = a] = 0 for all real numbers a, i.e.: the probability that X attains the value a is zero, for any number a. If the distribution of X is _____ then X is called a _____ random variable.
    a. Connectionist expert systems
    b. Decision tree pruning
    c. Pay Band
    d. Continuous

11. _____ is a management process whereby delivery (customer valued) processes are constantly evaluated and improved in the light of their efficiency, effectiveness and flexibility.

Some see it as a meta process for most management systems (Business Process Management, Quality Management, Project Management). Deming saw it as part of the 'system' whereby feedback from the process and customer were evaluated against organisational goals.

   a. First-mover advantage
   b. Critical Success Factor
   c. Sole proprietorship
   d. Continuous Improvement Process

12. _____ is the process of estimation in unknown situations. Prediction is a similar, but more general term. Both can refer to estimation of time series, cross-sectional or longitudinal data.
    a. 33 Strategies of War
    b. 28-hour day
    c. 1990 Clean Air Act
    d. Forecasting

Chapter 12. Sales and Operations Planning (Aggregate Planning)   75

13. _____ of the learning curve effect and the closely related experience curve effect express the relationship between equations for experience and efficiency or between efficiency gains and investment in the effort. The experience of 'learning curves' was first observed by the 19th Century German psychologist Hermann Ebbinghaus according to the difficulty of memorizing varying numbers of verbal stimuli, and subsequent learning about the complex processes of learning are discussed in the

The rule used for representing the learning curve effect states that the more times a task has been performed, the less time will be required on each subsequent iteration.

   a. Spatial Decision Support Systems
   b. Models
   c. Point biserial correlation coefficient
   d. Distribution

14. _____ is the process of understanding, anticipating and influencing consumer behavior in order to maximize revenue or profits from a fixed, perishable resource This process was first discovered by Dr. Matt H. Keller. The challenge is to sell the right resources to the right customer at the right time for the right price.
   a. Gap analysis
   b. Yield management
   c. Business model design
   d. Business networking

15. The _____ is the labour pool in employment. It is generally used to describe those working for a single company or industry, but can also apply to a geographic region like a city, country, state, etc. The term generally excludes the employers or management, and implies those involved in manual labour.
   a. Pink-collar worker
   b. Work-life balance
   c. Division of labour
   d. Workforce

16. A _____ is the system of organizations, people, technology, activities, information and resources involved in moving a product or service from supplier to customer. _____ activities transform natural resources, raw materials and components into a finished product that is delivered to the end customer. In sophisticated _____ systems, used products may re-enter the _____ at any point where residual value is recyclable.

Chapter 12. Sales and Operations Planning (Aggregate Planning)

a. Drop shipping
b. Packaging
c. Wholesalers
d. Supply chain

17. The function f is called, variously, an _____, cost function, energy function, or energy functional. A feasible solution that minimizes (or maximizes, if that is the goal) the _____ is called an optimal solution.

Generally, when the feasible region or the _____ of the problem does not present convexity, there may be several local minima and maxima, where a local minimum x^* is defined as a point for which there exists some $>\delta > 0$ so that for all x such that

$$\|x\|>$$

the expression

$$\|x\|>$$

holds; that is to say, on some region around x^* all of the function values are greater than or equal to the value at that point.

a. A Stake in the Outcome
b. Objective function
c. AAAI
d. A4e

18. A _____ is a set of instructions having the force of a directive, covering those features of operations that lend themselves to a definite or standardized procedure without loss of effectiveness. Standard Operating Policies and Procedures can be effective catalysts to drive performance improvement and improving organizational results.

a. Longitudinal study
b. Risk-benefit analysis
c. 1990 Clean Air Act
d. Standard operating procedure

19. _____ is the amount of inventory a company have in stock at the end of this fiscal year. It is closely related with _____ Cost, which is the amount of money spent to get these goods in stock. It should be calculated at the Lower of Cost or Market.

a. Ending inventory
b. A Stake in the Outcome
c. A4e
d. Inventory

Chapter 13. Managing Inventory throughout the Supply Chain

1. _____ is a term used by inventory specialists to describe a level of extra stock that is maintained below the cycle stock to buffer against stockouts. _____ exists to counter uncertainties in supply and demand. _____ is defined as extra units of inventory carried as protection against possible stockouts .(shortfall in raw material or packaging.)
   a. Safety stock
   b. Knowledge worker
   c. Process automation
   d. Product life cycle

2. In statistics and image processing, to smooth a data set is to create an approximating function that attempts to capture important patterns in the data, while leaving out noise or other fine-scale structures/rapid phenomena. Many different algorithms are used in _____. One of the most common algorithms is the 'moving average', often used to try to capture important trends in repeated statistical surveys.
   a. 1990 Clean Air Act
   b. 33 Strategies of War
   c. Smoothing
   d. 28-hour day

3. In economics, _____ is the desire to own something and the ability to pay for it. The term _____ signifies the ability or the willingness to buy a particular commodity at a given point of time.
   a. 28-hour day
   b. 33 Strategies of War
   c. 1990 Clean Air Act
   d. Demand

4. In probability theory, a probability distribution is called _____ if its cumulative distribution function is _____. This is equivalent to saying that for random variables X with the distribution in question, Pr[X = a] = 0 for all real numbers a, i.e.: the probability that X attains the value a is zero, for any number a. If the distribution of X is _____ then X is called a _____ random variable.
   a. Pay Band
   b. Decision tree pruning
   c. Connectionist expert systems
   d. Continuous

5. _____ is an advertisement in which a particular product specifically mentions a competitor by name for the express purpose of showing why the competitor is inferior to the product naming it.

This should not be confused with parody advertisements, where a fictional product is being advertised for the purpose of poking fun at the particular advertisement, nor should it be confused with the use of a coined brand name for the purpose of comparing the product without actually naming an actual competitor. ('Wikipedia tastes better and is less filling than the Encyclopedia Galactica.')

In the 1980s, during what has been referred to as the cola wars, soft-drink manufacturer Pepsi ran a series of advertisements where people, caught on hidden camera, in a blind taste test, chose Pepsi over rival Coca-Cola.

a. Comparative advertising
b. 33 Strategies of War
c. 28-hour day
d. 1990 Clean Air Act

6. _____ measures the performance of a system. Certain goals are defined and the _____ gives the percentage to which they should be achieved.

Examples

- Percentage of calls answered in a call center.
- Percentage of customers waiting less than a given fixed time.
- Percentage of customers that do not experience a stock out.

_____ is used in supply chain management and in inventory management to measure the performance of inventory systems.

Under stochastic conditions it is unavoidable that in some periods the inventory on hand is not sufficient to deliver the complete demand and, as a consequence, that part of the demand is filled only after an inventory-related waiting time.

a. 28-hour day
b. 1990 Clean Air Act
c. 33 Strategies of War
d. Service level

7. _____ is the level of inventory that minimizes the total inventory holding costs and ordering costs. The framework used to determine this order quantity is also known as Wilson _____ Model. The model was developed by F. W. Harris in 1913.

Chapter 13. Managing Inventory throughout the Supply Chain

   a. Effective executive
   b. Event management
   c. Anti-leadership
   d. Economic order quantity

8. The _____ is the level of inventory when a fresh order should be made with suppliers to bring the inventory up by the Economic order quantity ('EOQ'.)

The _____ for replenishment of stock occurs when the level of inventory drops down to zero. In view of instantaneous replenishment of stock the level of inventory jumps to the original level from zero level.

   a. 28-hour day
   b. Finished goods
   c. 1990 Clean Air Act
   d. Reorder point

9. _____ is an inventory strategy that strives to improve the return on investment of a business by reducing in-process inventory and its associated carrying costs. To meet _____ objectives, the process relies on signals between different points in the process. This means the process is often driven by a series of signals, or Kanban, which tell production when to make the next part. Kanban are usually 'tickets' but can be simple visual signals, such as the presence or absence of a part on a shelf. Implemented correctly, _____ can dramatically improve a manufacturing organization's return on investment, quality, and efficiency.
   a. Just-in-time
   b. 1990 Clean Air Act
   c. 33 Strategies of War
   d. 28-hour day

10. The _____ is an observed phenomenon in forecast-driven distribution channels. The concept has its roots in J Forrester's Industrial Dynamics (1961) and thus it is also known as the Forrester Effect. Since the oscillating demand magnification upstream a supply chain reminds someone of a cracking whip it became famous as the _____.
   a. Bullwhip effect
   b. 28-hour day
   c. 1990 Clean Air Act
   d. 33 Strategies of War

Chapter 13. Managing Inventory throughout the Supply Chain 81

11. A _____ is the system of organizations, people, technology, activities, information and resources involved in moving a product or service from supplier to customer. _____ activities transform natural resources, raw materials and components into a finished product that is delivered to the end customer. In sophisticated _____ systems, used products may re-enter the _____ at any point where residual value is recyclable.
   a. Drop shipping
   b. Wholesalers
   c. Packaging
   d. Supply chain

12. In marketing, _____ has come to mean the process by which marketers try to create an image or identity in the minds of their target market for its product, brand, or organization. It is the 'relative competitive comparison' their product occupies in a given market as perceived by the target market.

   Re-_____ involves changing the identity of a product, relative to the identity of competing products, in the collective minds of the target market.

   a. Customer analytics
   b. PEST analysis
   c. Context analysis
   d. Positioning

13. _____ is the science, art and technology of enclosing or protecting products for distribution, storage, sale, and use. _____ also refers to the process of design, evaluation, and production of packages. _____ can be described as a coordinated system of preparing goods for transport, warehousing, logistics, sale, and end use.
   a. Wholesalers
   b. Supply chain management
   c. Supply chain
   d. Packaging

14. In economics, business, retail, and accounting, a _____ is the value of money that has been used up to produce something, and hence is not available for use anymore. In economics, a _____ is an alternative that is given up as a result of a decision. In business, the _____ may be one of acquisition, in which case the amount of money expended to acquire it is counted as _____.
   a. Cost allocation
   b. Fixed costs
   c. Cost
   d. Cost overrun

Chapter 14. Managing Production across the Supply Chain

1. _____ is a business function that provides a response to customer order enquiries, based on resource availability. It generates available quantities of the requested product, and delivery due dates. Therefore, _____ supports order promising and fulfillment, aiming to manage demand and match it to production plans.
   a. A Stake in the Outcome
   b. A4e
   c. AAAI
   d. Available-to-promise

2. _____ is a software based production planning and inventory control system used to manage manufacturing processes. Although it is not common nowadays, it is possible to conduct _____ by hand as well.

An _____ system is intended to simultaneously meet three objectives:

   - Ensure materials and products are available for production and delivery to customers.
   - Maintain the lowest possible level of inventory.
   - Plan manufacturing activities, delivery schedules and purchasing activities.

Manufacturing organizations, whatever their products, face the same daily practical problem - that customers want products to be available in a shorter time than it takes to make them. This means that some level of planning is required.

   a. Material requirements planning
   b. 33 Strategies of War
   c. 1990 Clean Air Act
   d. 28-hour day

3. _____ is an integrated business management process through which the executive/leadership team continually achieves focus, alignment and synchronization among all the functions of the organization. The monthly S'OP plan includes an updated sales plan, production plan, inventory plan, customer lead time (backlog) plan, new product development plan, strategic initiative plan and resulting financial plan. Done well, the S'OP process also enables effective supply chain management.
   a. 28-hour day
   b. 1990 Clean Air Act
   c. 33 Strategies of War
   d. Sales and operations planning

4. _____ is one of the managerial functions like planning, organizing, staffing and directing. It is an important function because it helps to check the errors and to take the corrective action so that deviation from standards are minimized and stated goals of the organization are achieved in desired manner. According to modern concepts, _____ is a foreseeing action whereas earlier concept of _____ was used only when errors were detected. _____ in management means setting standards, measuring actual performance and taking corrective action.

Chapter 14. Managing Production across the Supply Chain

a. Turnover
b. Control
c. Schedule of reinforcement
d. Decision tree pruning

5. In economics, _____ is the desire to own something and the ability to pay for it. The term _____ signifies the ability or the willingness to buy a particular commodity at a given point of time.
   a. 1990 Clean Air Act
   b. 33 Strategies of War
   c. 28-hour day
   d. Demand

6. _____ is the amount of inventory a company have in stock at the end of this fiscal year. It is closely related with _____ Cost, which is the amount of money spent to get these goods in stock. It should be calculated at the Lower of Cost or Market.
   a. Inventory
   b. A4e
   c. A Stake in the Outcome
   d. Ending inventory

7. A _____ is a plan for production, staffing, inventory, etc. It is usually linked to manufacturing where the plan indicates when and how much of each product will be demanded. This plan quantifies significant processes, parts, and other resources in order to optimize production, to identify bottlenecks, and to anticipate needs and completed goods.
   a. Piecework
   b. Remanufacturing
   c. Master production schedule
   d. Value engineering

8. The _____ is the amount of time an organization will look into the future when preparing a strategic plan. Many commercial companies use a five-year _____, but other organizations such as the Forestry Commission in the UK have to use a much longer _____ to form effective plans.
   a. No-bid contract
   b. Psychological pricing
   c. Strategic Alliance
   d. Planning horizon

Chapter 14. Managing Production across the Supply Chain

9. _____ is a list of the raw materials, sub-assemblies, intermediate assemblies, sub-components, components, parts and the quantities of each needed to manufacture an end item (final product).
   a. Methods-time measurement
   b. Piece rate
   c. Scientific management
   d. Bill of materials

10. _____ is the process of determining the production capacity needed by an organization to meet changing demands for its products. In the context of _____, 'capacity' is the maximum amount of work that an organization is capable of completing in a given period of time.

    A discrepancy between the capacity of an organization and the demands of its customers results in inefficiency, either in under-utilized resources or unfulfilled customers.

   a. Scientific management
   b. Capacity planning
   c. Productivity
   d. Remanufacturing

11. A _____ is the period of time between the initiation of any process of production and the completion of that process. Thus the _____ for ordering a new car from a manufacturer may be anywhere from 2 weeks to 6 months. In industry, _____ reduction is an important part of lean manufacturing.
   a. 33 Strategies of War
   b. 1990 Clean Air Act
   c. 28-hour day
   d. Lead time

12. _____ is the use of an object (typically referred to as an RFID tag) applied to or incorporated into a product, animal, or person for the purpose of identification and tracking using radio waves. Some tags can be read from several meters away and beyond the line of sight of the reader.

    Most RFID tags contain at least two parts.

   a. 28-hour day
   b. 33 Strategies of War
   c. 1990 Clean Air Act
   d. Radio-frequency identification

Chapter 14. Managing Production across the Supply Chain

13. A _____ is the system of organizations, people, technology, activities, information and resources involved in moving a product or service from supplier to customer. _____ activities transform natural resources, raw materials and components into a finished product that is delivered to the end customer. In sophisticated _____ systems, used products may re-enter the _____ at any point where residual value is recyclable.
    a. Drop shipping
    b. Packaging
    c. Supply chain
    d. Wholesalers

14. _____ is one of the four elements of marketing mix. An organization or set of organizations (go-betweens) involved in the process of making a product or service available for use or consumption by a consumer or business user.

The other three parts of the marketing mix are product, pricing, and promotion.

   a. Missing completely at random
   b. Distribution
   c. Job creation programs
   d. Matching theory

Chapter 15. JIT/Lean Production

1. _____ is an inventory strategy that strives to improve the return on investment of a business by reducing in-process inventory and its associated carrying costs. To meet _____ objectives, the process relies on signals between different points in the process. This means the process is often driven by a series of signals, or Kanban, which tell production when to make the next part. Kanban are usually 'tickets' but can be simple visual signals, such as the presence or absence of a part on a shelf. Implemented correctly, _____ can dramatically improve a manufacturing organization's return on investment, quality, and efficiency.
   a. 1990 Clean Air Act
   b. Just-in-time
   c. 33 Strategies of War
   d. 28-hour day

2. _____ or lean production, which is often known simply as 'Lean', is a production practice that considers the expenditure of resources for any goal other than the creation of value for the end customer to be wasteful, and thus a target for elimination. Working from the perspective of the customer who consumes a product or service, 'value' is defined as any action or process that a customer would be willing to pay for. Basically, lean is centered around creating more value with less work.
   a. Theory of constraints
   b. Production line
   c. Six Sigma
   d. Lean manufacturing

3. _____ is a concept related to lean and just-in-time (JIT) production. The Japanese word _____ is a common term meaning 'signboard' or 'billboard'. According to Taiichi Ohno, the man credited with developing JIT, _____ is a means through which JIT is achieved.
   a. Kanban
   b. Trademark
   c. Risk management
   d. Succession planning

4. A _____ is the system of organizations, people, technology, activities, information and resources involved in moving a product or service from supplier to customer. _____ activities transform natural resources, raw materials and components into a finished product that is delivered to the end customer. In sophisticated _____ systems, used products may re-enter the _____ at any point where residual value is recyclable.
   a. Drop shipping
   b. Packaging
   c. Supply chain
   d. Wholesalers

Chapter 15. JIT/Lean Production

5. _____ is a software based production planning and inventory control system used to manage manufacturing processes. Although it is not common nowadays, it is possible to conduct _____ by hand as well.

An _____ system is intended to simultaneously meet three objectives:

- Ensure materials and products are available for production and delivery to customers.
- Maintain the lowest possible level of inventory.
- Plan manufacturing activities, delivery schedules and purchasing activities.

Manufacturing organizations, whatever their products, face the same daily practical problem - that customers want products to be available in a shorter time than it takes to make them. This means that some level of planning is required.

a. 33 Strategies of War
b. Material requirements planning
c. 1990 Clean Air Act
d. 28-hour day

Chapter 16. Managing Information Technologies across the Supply Chain

1. A _____ is the system of organizations, people, technology, activities, information and resources involved in moving a product or service from supplier to customer. _____ activities transform natural resources, raw materials and components into a finished product that is delivered to the end customer. In sophisticated _____ systems, used products may re-enter the _____ at any point where residual value is recyclable.
   a. Packaging
   b. Drop shipping
   c. Wholesalers
   d. Supply chain

2. _____ can be regarded as an outcome of mental processes (cognitive process) leading to the selection of a course of action among several alternatives. Every _____ process produces a final choice. The output can be an action or an opinion of choice.
   a. 33 Strategies of War
   b. 1990 Clean Air Act
   c. 28-hour day
   d. Decision making

3. _____ consists of the processes a company uses to track and organize its contacts with its current and prospective customers. _____ software is used to support these processes; information about customers and customer interactions can be entered, stored and accessed by employees in different company departments. Typical _____ goals are to improve services provided to customers, and to use customer contact information for targeted marketing.
   a. Green marketing
   b. Disruptive technology
   c. Marketing plan
   d. Customer relationship management

4. _____ constitute a class of computer-based information systems including knowledge-based systems that support decision-making activities.

   _____ are a specific class of computerized information systems that supports business and organizational decision-making activities. A properly-designed _____ is an interactive software-based system intended to help decision makers compile useful information from raw data, documents, personal knowledge, and/or business models to identify and solve problems and make decisions.

   a. Decision support systems
   b. 28-hour day
   c. Spatial Decision Support Systems
   d. 1990 Clean Air Act

Chapter 16. Managing Information Technologies across the Supply Chain 89

5. _____ is an integrated business management process through which the executive/leadership team continually achieves focus, alignment and synchronization among all the functions of the organization. The monthly S'OP plan includes an updated sales plan, production plan, inventory plan, customer lead time (backlog) plan, new product development plan, strategic initiative plan and resulting financial plan. Done well, the S'OP process also enables effective supply chain management.
   a. 33 Strategies of War
   b. Sales and operations planning
   c. 1990 Clean Air Act
   d. 28-hour day

6. _____ is the management of a network of interconnected businesses involved in the ultimate provision of product and service packages required by end customers (Harland, 1996.) _____ spans all movement and storage of raw materials, work-in-process inventory, and finished goods from point of origin to point of consumption (supply chain.)

   The definition an American professional association put forward is that _____ encompasses the planning and management of all activities involved in sourcing, procurement, conversion, and logistics management activities.

   a. Drop shipping
   b. Packaging
   c. Freight forwarder
   d. Supply chain management

7. _____ is a statistical technique in decision making that is used for selection of a limited number of tasks that produce significant overall effect. It uses the Pareto principle - the idea that by doing 20% of work you can generate 80% of the advantage of doing the entire job. Or in terms of quality improvement, a large majority of problems (80%) are produced by a few key causes (20%.)
   a. Polychoric correlation
   b. Goodness of fit
   c. Pareto analysis
   d. Probability matching

8. _____ ('Plan-Do-Check-Act') is an iterative four-step problem-solving process typically used in business process improvement. It is also known as the Deming Cycle, Shewhart cycle, Deming Wheel, or Plan-Do-Study-Act.

   _____ was made popular by Dr. W. Edwards Deming, who is considered by many to be the father of modern quality control; however it was always referred to by him as the Shewhart cycle. Later in Deming's career, he modified _____ to Plan, Do, Study, Act (PDSA) so as to better describe his recommendations.

Chapter 16. Managing Information Technologies across the Supply Chain

a. Management team
b. Decentralization
c. Management by exception
d. PDCA

9. The _____ of an edge is $c_f(u, v) = c(u, v) - f(u, v)$. This defines a residual network denoted $G_f(V, \overline{E_f})$, giving the amount of available capacity. See that there can be an edge from u to v in the residual network, even though there is no edge from u to v in the original network.

a. 33 Strategies of War
b. Residual capacity
c. 1990 Clean Air Act
d. 28-hour day

10. _____ is the management of the flow of goods, information and other resources, including energy and people, between the point of origin and the point of consumption in order to meet the requirements of consumers (frequently, and originally, military organizations.) _____ involves the integration of information, transportation, inventory, warehousing, material-handling, and packaging, and occasionally security. _____ is a channel of the supply chain which adds the value of time and place utility.

a. 1990 Clean Air Act
b. Third-party logistics
c. 28-hour day
d. Logistics

11. _____ is a company-wide computer software system used to manage and coordinate all the resources, information, and functions of a business from shared data stores.

An _____ system has a service-oriented architecture with modular hardware and software units and 'services' that communicate on a local area network. The modular design allows a business to add or reconfigure modules (perhaps from different vendors) while preserving data integrity in one shared database that may be centralized or distributed.

a. AAAI
b. A Stake in the Outcome
c. A4e
d. Enterprise resource planning

Chapter 16. Managing Information Technologies across the Supply Chain

12. A _____ is a commercial building for storage of goods. _____s are used by manufacturers, importers, exporters, wholesalers, transport businesses, customs, etc. They are usually large plain buildings in industrial areas of cities and towns.

   a. 33 Strategies of War
   b. Warehouse
   c. 1990 Clean Air Act
   d. 28-hour day

13. In marketing, _____ has come to mean the process by which marketers try to create an image or identity in the minds of their target market for its product, brand, or organization. It is the 'relative competitive comparison' their product occupies in a given market as perceived by the target market.

   Re-_____ involves changing the identity of a product, relative to the identity of competing products, in the collective minds of the target market.

   a. Context analysis
   b. Customer analytics
   c. PEST analysis
   d. Positioning

ANSWER KEY

Chapter 1
1. c   2. c   3. a   4. b   5. d   6. d   7. c   8. b   9. c   10. c
11. d   12. c   13. a   14. d   15. d   16. a   17. d   18. c   19. c   20. d
21. d   22. d

Chapter 2
1. d   2. d   3. b   4. d   5. a   6. c   7. d   8. c   9. c   10. c
11. b   12. c   13. b   14. d   15. d   16. d

Chapter 3
1. b   2. d   3. b   4. b   5. b   6. d   7. d   8. d   9. b   10. b
11. d   12. c   13. c   14. d   15. d   16. a

Chapter 4
1. d   2. a   3. a   4. d   5. d   6. d   7. d   8. a   9. c   10. d
11. d   12. d   13. b   14. b   15. d   16. d   17. b   18. a   19. b   20. b
21. d   22. d   23. b   24. d   25. c   26. d   27. c   28. d   29. d   30. c
31. d   32. d   33. d

Chapter 5
1. a   2. d   3. d   4. b   5. b   6. d

Chapter 6
1. b   2. a   3. c   4. b   5. d   6. d   7. a   8. a   9. d   10. d
11. d   12. d   13. d

Chapter 7
1. d   2. a   3. d   4. d   5. b   6. d   7. d   8. d   9. d   10. a
11. b   12. d   13. c   14. b

Chapter 8
1. d   2. c   3. d   4. b   5. d   6. b   7. c   8. c   9. c   10. d
11. d   12. d   13. d

Chapter 9
1. b   2. b   3. d   4. d   5. d   6. a   7. d   8. d   9. d   10. b
11. b   12. b   13. d   14. b   15. b   16. c   17. a   18. c

Chapter 10
1. d   2. b   3. a   4. d   5. d   6. d   7. d   8. d   9. d   10. d
11. d   12. b   13. d   14. d   15. d   16. d   17. a   18. c   19. d   20. b
21. d   22. b   23. c   24. a   25. a   26. d   27. c   28. d   29. d   30. d
31. d   32. b

ANSWER KEY

Chapter 11
1. d 2. d 3. d 4. d 5. b 6. d 7. d 8. b 9. b 10. d
11. d 12. d 13. c 14. a 15. b 16. a 17. d 18. a 19. a 20. b
21. b 22. d

Chapter 12
1. b 2. b 3. c 4. c 5. d 6. d 7. b 8. b 9. a 10. d
11. d 12. d 13. b 14. b 15. d 16. d 17. b 18. d 19. a

Chapter 13
1. a 2. c 3. d 4. d 5. a 6. d 7. d 8. d 9. a 10. a
11. d 12. d 13. d 14. c

Chapter 14
1. d 2. a 3. d 4. b 5. d 6. d 7. c 8. d 9. d 10. b
11. d 12. d 13. c 14. b

Chapter 15
1. b 2. d 3. a 4. c 5. b

Chapter 16
1. d 2. d 3. d 4. a 5. b 6. d 7. c 8. d 9. b 10. d
11. d 12. b 13. d

www.ingramcontent.com/pod-product-compliance
Lightning Source LLC
Chambersburg PA
CBHW081846230426
43669CB00018B/2843